GRAMMAR WARS

179 Games and Improvs for Learning Language Arts

Tom Ready

MERIWETHER PUBLISHING LTD.
Colorado Springs, Colorado

Meriwether Publishing Ltd., Publisher
P.O. Box 7710
Colorado Springs, CO 80933

Executive editor: Theodore O. Zapel
Assistant editor: Jennifer Vokolek McAloon
Typesetting: Elisabeth Hendricks
Cover design: Janice Melvin

Library of Congress Cataloging-in-Publication Data

Ready, Tom, date.
    Grammar wars : 179 games and improvs for learning language arts / Tom Ready.
      p. cm.
    ISBN 1-56608-063-0 (pbk.)
    1. English language--Grammar--Study and teaching. 2. Language arts.
  3. Drama in education. 4. Educational games. I. Title.

    LB1575.8 .R39 2000
    808'.042'071--dc21

                                            00-041127

1 2 3 4 5   00 01 02 03

Acknowledgments

Over the past several years, numerous friends and colleagues have assisted in different ways in supporting the integration of improvisational games and the language arts standards. First of all, I want to thank Jane, "Haf," and the California Arts Project for the time, resources, and opportunities each has made available to me over the past decade, allowing me to experiment and explore. Much appreciation to my NCAP team — Steve, Jan, Steve, Denise, Stacey, Virginia, Joe, and David — for the caliber of work that set the standard for this and other projects we've undertaken. A belated applause for the Christa McAuliffe program for its support for the year of work with K-8 schools in the northern California area that made the fun and field-testing possible. Thanks to the various improvisation teachers in public education in northern California, and Rebecca Stockley and the folks at Bay Area Theatresports™ for their constant and stimulating work.

To all my acting classes at Lassen High School, especially the Advanced Drama classes (Jason, Isaac, Brian, Jodi, DJ, Tony, Levi, Steve, Paul, Becky, Erin, MOB and Mindy), thanks for the learning environment you provided.

Most importantly, thanks to my family: Karen, Nick, and Melissa, for the patience and freedom you have given me over the past few years at school and away from home to play with the ideas that led to this book.

Contents

Introduction

Background

In my own education, I learned the grammar and parts of speech that got me through high school when I took Spanish as a foreign language in my middle school years in New York. Perhaps I absorbed some things in this class because the woman scared me so much. But she had no choice: We had to learn grammar in order to put the syntax together because we could only speak in Spanish. Sink or swim.

I got through my undergraduate work in the University of California and the California State University systems with instincts from having grown up speaking English, and from instincts about where to "pause" and throw in a comma.

On a parallel track I began taking speech and acting classes, and there I finally found an area where my interests focused and thrived. Performance presented language to me in a way that made words physical things, that made syntax something musical with shifting dynamics and rhythm. Working with language on-stage, along with the body and face as accompanying instruments, made language and communication oddly captivating, and a little like an emotional roller-coaster.

When I began teaching English and drama, I found myself having to learn more about the nuts and bolts of the language in order to teach it and seem informed when any of my students asked me questions. Maybe because I was older, or maybe because I was now having to teach grammar, parts of speech, and punctuation, I found the whole thing quite simple, or at least the basic concepts involved.

So off I went with my students working in a traditional way, teaching the editing skills that would hopefully let their writing skills fit smoothly into the flow of standard conventions expected in post-secondary and employment arenas.

Grammar, punctuation, parts of speech

In two decades of teaching English, I have had the opportunity to work with a number of English teachers. In that time the Literature Based Instruction Model arrived and seemed to be received with open arms by many book-loving instructors. Now, along with the call to teach editing skills "in context" of the students' own writings, teachers had a mandate that could justify an overemphasis on teaching books that "I've always loved, and the students should, too." Such teaching from the heart of one's own experience certainly is a wonderful motivating factor, making it possible to infuse in kids a love of reading. However, I suspect that there was a silent and unadvertised acceptance that now we didn't have to attack the less inspired instruction on editing skills involving grammar, punctuation, and parts of speech.

It was too mechanical, mathematical, and uninspiring. After all, most important was getting the students to have something important or passionate to say: content before form.

Competitive improvisation

The more I taught English and drama simultaneously, the more the parallels between the two grew in my mind. What I experienced but didn't consciously understand in college was the essential sameness of language performed and language written, between rehearsal and reading. What writers do with paper and pen, actors do in time and space with their bodies, faces and voices. Whatever appears on the page has its stage equivalent, and vice versa.

In the early '90s I attended a workshop for teachers where a woman who taught improvisation in northern California presented exercises for training and competition derived from Keith Johnstone's work in England and Canada under the name of Theatresports™. The short demonstration was crisp, energetic and lively. The book *Improvisation Through Theatresports*™ was recommended that had been written by two women in San Francisco who worked with the Bay Area Theatresports™ (BATS).

What I discovered was a huge, growing network of improvisational actors from all over the world, all of whom were generating their own repertoire of improvisational exercises and games that were showing up in books and on web pages throughout the Internet.

In my acting classes at the high school, in the community, and in workshops conducted in the state prisons, I saw exercises using language in creative and entertaining ways, many times in ways that blurred the line between performance and language practice for academic instructional purposes. Was this an acting class or an English class?

Since that dawning about how the nature of each separate discipline could be used to teach the other, I've used improvisation to teach English, and English standards to teach effective rehearsal and performance skills.

What follows is a listing of exercises and games that can be used to introduce, teach or assess students' learning in at least the areas of punctuation, grammar, and parts of speech. Feel free to disagree with the placements of certain activities at certain levels. If you are a teacher, you will know your students well enough to be able to choose and modify the exercises to make them productive for your objectives. Similarly, you might see that any of the games might be converted in some way to serve another content standard from English or any other discipline. Super! Many of the games' structures I refer to as "Empty buckets." The games are just an activity into which you put an instructional objective: You drive the activity with whatever objective you have to meet.

Preparing Your Class: Team-building and Risk-taking
Preparing the teacher

The very nature of using *Grammar Wars* as a method will draw some teachers and repel others. Some instructors are physical and creative, while others might be a bit more serious and controlled in their personal qualities. After all, "English is an academic subject and should be treated seriously."

I respect that thinking. Furthermore, I know there's a danger in simply doing these exercises with your classes, because there is the real danger that the students will sooner or later enjoy doing them. The fatal result is that everyone might assume that the students are learning. Certainly we fool the administrative evaluator who completes his or her ten-minute evaluation of your professional effectiveness for the entire year when your students are actively performing these games, using and critiquing the content knowledge and skills required.

The purpose of this method is to provide an energetic vehicle that students want to do, that students enjoy, that invites the practice and repetition that is needed to get facts and skills to become ingrained in their minds. The purpose is to build into the students the knowledge of language and the composition skills that will make them like language, and that will make them code and decode effectively when they leave our schools.

Preparing the students

I have heard some teachers state that children have excellent imaginations early on in school, but eventually, for a myriad of reasons, they become self-conscious, get focused on correct and incorrect answer thinking, and begin to distrust play and creation. I know that in my drama classes, where some students are taking their first fine art class ever, I have to make great efforts to lay a foundation of emotional safety between the students. Similarly, I have to monitor my own statements and behavior to ensure that I am seen as an advocate while I am simultaneously conducting the exercises that are threatening their security.

If the students have not been involved in a fine arts curriculum, or have not enjoyed teachers who have a spirit of play in their classrooms, your work might best begin by using the exercises that seem the safest as students perform for their peers, and safest in terms of chances for success. I personally have found great success in using the lower level exercises with my high school students. They might sense the simplicity of the exercise and be unsure or embarrassed, but if I participate or demonstrate and have fun, then they usually come along willingly.

In the middle school grades, core teachers might have an advantage in being able to use their time and methods in an integrated fashion. Combining social studies, language arts and drama is a common practice I've seen with various colleagues in northern California. Taking the time and exploring the advantages of the *Grammar Wars* approach might provide an ongoing activity to use information from all three subject areas to apply, explore, and reinforce important facts and skills.

In high school, students can fall anywhere in the range of willingness, from those who volunteer too often, to those who are way too "cool" to participate. I have had students with abilities in special education to advanced placement participate effectively and horridly. It doesn't seem to have as much to do with academic ability as emotional stability, confidence and fear. If a good, supportive environment can be established, then sooner rather than later, everyone will participate willingly.

Review two of the texts identified in the Resources section of this book, one by Belt and Stockley, the other by Viola Spolin, for activities and warm-ups to get students having fun with words and language, moving into creative and spontaneous play. I like to use "Yes, and ..." and "Q and A" for simple spontaneity and group creation. "Word at a Time" exercises also prepare the students for group creations that at the same time reinforce to the students that they only have to (or get to) contribute part of the time. Offer a little, accept a little and watch what we can create together.

Improv Concepts

There are a couple of important concepts in improvisation that might help the instructor prepare the groundwork for a class to be willing to "play" in these games. This is the case especially in a school program where the students have moved through several grades without creativity curricula, specifically in drama where both imaginative movement and the use of language operate naturally together.

Offering

When a player "offers" in an empty space, he or she is essentially creating something simply by speaking the words (e.g., "Is that your dog?"). Offers can also be made via questions despite the uncertainty that characterizes a question (For example, the question, "Will you tell me what she said?" creates a girl character somewhere, and an earlier conversation, though no third character is onstage).

Accepting

When a second actor hears and continues to speak about or physically work with an earlier offer, he is said to "accept" the offer. Children do this naturally and quickly, but without such "play" being socially or academically acceptable, students can learn to fear such behavior. This imaginative exchange becomes "stupid," or something that "cool" people don't do. All this despite the fact that people today spend countless hours and money entertaining themselves by watching professional actors and politicians earn their livelihoods by engaging in such behaviors.

Where to begin

Because language only became interesting to me in college when I started acting and doing speeches, I feel comfortable introducing students to language as a physical "thing." Words convey pictures and events of things and actions in narration, so kids can be encouraged to "see" this representational concept by acting. What they can read, they can act out: conversely, what they can do, they can then record in writing.

Brian Way in his book, *Development through Drama*, gives a rationale and ideas for early education using some of the simplest and safest ideas in creative dramatics. Viola Spolin's *Improvisation for the Theater* presents hundreds of activities that introduce and motivate young actors to produce as performers, setting the stage for them to effectively "play" *Grammar Wars* activities. The benefit of beginning in a simple and rudimentary way is that the basics of drama have extensive parallels with effective writing and reading. I have been struck over the years at the similarity between acting rehearsals and developmental reading instruction where "purpose" determines the goal of reading and the time needed to complete it successfully. One discipline serves the other.

The book that I have used over the past five or so years, *Improvisation through Theatresports™*, was written by Rebecca Stockley and Linda Belt out of the Bay Area Theatresports™ (BATS) improv school. This text might not have a lot of exercises that are immediately useful for the lower levels, but in the higher grades, the ideas and options are plentiful. For anyone who takes the opportunity to attend a live improvisational tournament, you might find that the focus of the scene work hinges around narrative and characterization, rather than the academic focus that dominates *Grammar Wars* with its focus on punctuation, grammar, and parts of speech.

A final resource, if you are not one to "dive" into drama, would be to contact a theatre person in your community or in the public school system. Such an individual might be best for introducing you to content, techniques and methods that will get your students to play and create without judgment and fear of being "wrong" or doing something "incorrectly."

Note

The exercises suggested here and in the resources for competitive improv are too difficult to do perfectly: They invite error. Let me say that again: The exercises suggested here and in the resources for competitive improv are too difficult to do perfectly: They invite error. That's OK. With the class or audience watching; with the demand to do the scene, listen to your partner, and physically work the environment; and with the *Grammar Wars* requirement of having to use this punctuation or not to use this part of speech, there are just too many balls in the air to juggle perfectly. And, indeed, if the actors were able to do it without flaw, the presentation would lose its entertainment value. We want to see our heroes suffer. These exercises do just that.

Part of the training, then, must be the understanding that as a team we will all succeed and flop. Just like life. But since we all know that, and since we will all experience the successes and flops together, we are all in the same boat. We are all part of one team learning together, trying the impossible over and over—and having a marvelous time in the process. If the teacher can lay the groundwork for that kind of safety, then the students will play, learn, and support each other.

And will they ever have a good time learning.

Conducting a Competition

Once your class or team is comfortable with the games you've introduced and practiced with them, and once they have a working facility with the content and performance standards served, then you have a good groundwork to conduct a small competition or tournament in class or for an outside audience.

Create teams from the class roster. I recommend that you change the composition of each team regularly so that the members see the class as the real team, the ensemble. It can be dangerous to tolerate a burgeoning clique that can become exclusive and promote negative feelings in the class. Some students will pursue winning at the expense of the corporate unity, and ultimately that will dampen energy and creativity. Back to worksheets.

Depending on your grade level and the students' critical abilities, you can either be the judge yourself, or you can use a team of student judges. Sometimes the scoring is easy because correct guesses earn a point, and so at the end of a round, the task is simply which team has more points. With some games, however, the judges need to have a broader knowledge of language because participants will come up with the unique, brilliant, or "the exception." Also, sometimes the vote falls closely toward the subjective choice. In this case, using "blind ballots" may be useful: The class can vote for whomever they believe performed the best without falling to peer pressure. Or, the teacher may choose to cast the deciding vote.

For theatre people who are familiar with Creative Dramatics and the work of Brian Way in England, it is worth considering that performances or formal competitions do not have to take place with an audience at all. Students profit from the creative work and the ensemble creative process. There is profit in the process experience, and having an audience is just one option. Fledgling performers might really like this idea a lot.

Rounds can involve having both teams play games for a certain amount of time. Other options might involve a round involving a specific number of games, perhaps an odd number so that ties can be avoided. Teachers can set up a familiar tournament bracket to chart the progress of the teams.

If these "competitions" are conducted regularly, and teams are constantly being made and dissolved so that the real team is the class, then kids will support and applaud good work when they see it, whether from their own team members or from the team against whom they are competing. In either case, good improvisers support all the actors regardless of the team on which they compete. I like to encourage the opposing team to lead the applause when the other team has finished an exercise.

Again, in a strongly supportive environment risk, learning, creativity and joy are always present. So competitions need to be manicured to continue what you have been working to create in the learning environment from the very beginning.

Author's Note

Several of the games in this book require the teacher and student to have knowledge of the dramatic "Form." What is "The Form"?

Let's start off with what it is not. English teachers will often approach teaching narrative structure with the following terms: exposition, complication, conflict, rising action, crisis, climax, and falling action. With those elements pretty strictly followed, or with some stylistic shifts here or there in that structure, most authors and playwrights stick closely to that template. At least it's a good starting point to note the basic similarities, and then variations on that form that distinguish creative writers.

When doing improv scenes or longer forms, the average improviser might find that remembering seven terms might be too much to hold in your head while you are also playing the scene itself and trying to work the requirements of the grammar game.

Way too much.

Here is what "The Form" is.

In improv, there's a let's-go-camping-and-pack-light version, or a *Reader's Digest* template that boils down the academic, seven-part template to four basic parts. And I think it'll surprise you how effective it is. I call it "The Form." The terms come from Keith Johnstone's book, *IMPRO*. (Read it if you are a teacher; it's a trip.)

The terms are pretty good in that they are almost self-explanatory:

Routine
Problem
Solution
New Routine

Here's the explanation. The hero opens the story with a life that is in its *Routine* phase. Now this might be a wonderful condition or pattern, but it's cyclical and what our hero is coping with. Now that *Routine* gets interrupted with a *Problem* of some sort. So, the hero has to go about finding a *Solution* to the *Problem*, preferably from the raw material in the *Routine* phase of the story. Once the *Problem* is solved, the hero is inevitably changed (dynamic character) by the experience, and he or she goes back to a pattern; however, because the hero is changed the final pattern is somehow different and is therefore a *New Routine*.

Let's look at a simple example I'll make up based on something that happened to me today:

ROUTINE: Tom got through the morning with the usual tasks of waking, showering, eating, and getting off to school. He kissed his wife, and then quietly said good-bye to his sleeping children, Nick and Melissa. He grabbed his briefcase, hopped in the truck, and drove off to school.

PROBLEM: As he was driving down the street toward the high school, he noticed a clicking and then a screeching sound coming from his engine or clutch. He pulled over to let the engine idle for a moment. Thinking that the sound might have been just a cold morning fluke, he pressed down on the clutch. Metal screamed, the truck lurched, and the engine died.

Tom had no time to deal with the dead vehicle and no cell phone to call for help, so being only three blocks from the school, he grabbed his case and began to walk.

SOLUTION: At lunch he called a tow truck to take the vehicle to the shop, and then called home to get one of his kids to pick him up from school at the end of the day. When he called at lunch, a groggy voice answered.

"Can you pick me up after school and take me to the shop?"

"I have plans today," said the waking voice.

"Do you want to pay your own car insurance?" Tom asked calmly.

"I'll be there at four."

NEW ROUTINE: The next morning Tom woke up, showered and ate, and kissed his wife good-bye. He then went quietly to the bedroom doors of his children's rooms, told them to get up, out of bed, into the shower, and eat.

He also mentioned that a list of chores for each of them was taped to the refrigerator door. Tom got in his truck and drove off, expecting a thoroughly wonderful day ahead of him.

Games and Improvs

ABCs

Easy

1. Lead Letter

Setup: Players or teams are given a letter.

A
Apple
Alligator
Arkansas
Ant

Process: Either verbally on demand, or with twenty seconds to prepare, the competitor presents as many words as possible beginning with that letter.

Scoring: Player or team with most words wins.

Easy

2. Alphabetize

Setup: Competing players are given a stack of five to ten words.

Process: Each is to put words in alphabetical order. Younger levels may sequence by the first letters.

Example: Apple, Mountain, Zebra

Older levels might have words in which the determining letters are further on in the words.

Example: Sequence, Sequencing, Sequential

Scoring: Fastest wins.

Easy

3. Start with a Letter (or End with a Letter)

(End with a Letter and the story example go up the grade levels.)

Setup: Player is given a letter.

Process: Player must speak a sentence that begins with that letter, and/or player is given a letter and must tell a story only with sentences that begin (or end) with that letter.

15

Scoring: An elimination (spelling bee) format works best — if correctly done, the player goes to the end of the line to wait their turn to compete again. If incorrect, they must go to their seat. Last competitor standing wins.

Easy

4. Upper-Lower Case

Setup: With big butcher paper or a chalkboard with writing lines (a solid lower and upper line with the dotted middle line), a player is verbally (or by sight) given a letter.

Process: The player writes an upper case and a lower case of the letter.

Scoring: When done, the time is noted along with the correctness of the penmanship. Penalties for errors. Scores of competing players determine the winner.

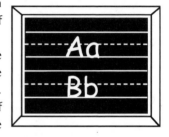

Easy

5. Loud Letters

Setup: Player is handed five to ten cards with letters on them. Reproducible "ABC" cards (upper and lower case) are on pages 103-115. Vowels (short and long) are on pages 116-118.

Process: Player has thirty to sixty seconds to pronounce the correct sounds associated with that letter. For vowels, either one or both of the appropriate sounds (short or long) are required. Can use blends, too.

Scoring: An elimination (spelling bee) format works best — if correctly done, the player goes to the end of the line to wait their turn to compete again. If incorrect, they must go to their seat. Last competitor standing wins.

6. Alphabet Pairs

Setup: Two players from each team go to the front.

Process: For Letters — They are to alternate saying the letters of the alphabet from A to Z. For Words — They are to alternate saying words, the first letters of which go in alphabetical sequence from A to Z. For Sentences — They are to alternate saying sentences. The first letter of the first word of each sentence goes in alphabetical sequence from A to Z.

Scoring: The activity is timed and the fastest pair wins.

7. Spell-Well Letter Number

Setup: Two players from opposing teams come to the front. The facilitator gets a number from one to five from the audience.

Process: One player begins by saying a word that has at least the number of letters as the number obtained from the audience. The second player then has to say another word that begins with the letter in the word just stated that is the same number in the sequence of letters given by the audience.

For example, the audience says, "3."

Player A: Mo**n**key. ("n" is the #3 letter, so ...)

Player B: Nu**p**tial. ("p" is the #3 letter, so ...)

Player A: Psychologist (etc.)

Scoring: The first player to make a mistake is "out" and the other competitor is the winner.

Easy

8. All Together Now!

Setup: The team stands together in the front of the room. The facilitator gives a three- or four-letter word.

Process: The team must simultaneously say the letters in the word aloud, correctly and in order.

Scoring: Each team continues with different words until all but one team is eliminated.

 Easy

9. Mix a Spell

Setup: Player goes to the front of the class and is given either chalk or a set of cards with the needed letters (and number of each letter) for the game. Reproducible "ABC" cards are on pages 103-115. Prior to the competition a group of words has been agreed upon (the vocabulary words for the week/month/semester, or "irregular" words — e.g., was, were, says, said, who, what, why).

Process: When the word to spell is given, the player must un-mix the letters in the stack (or spell with chalk) and spell the word correctly.

Scoring: An elimination (spelling bee) format works best — if correctly done, the player goes to the end of the line to wait their turn to compete again. If incorrect, they must go to their seat. Last competitor standing wins.

 Easy

10. Alphabet Scramble

Setup: Two players from one team go to the front where there is a data table (chalkboard, felt cloth, or chart on the floor) of perhaps five boxes across and six boxes down. (Any format is good as long as there are at least 26 boxes.) The team is also handed flash cards with the letters of the alphabet on them, mixed up. Reproducible alphabet flash cards are on pages 103-115.

Process: Being timed, the team of two is to set in order (left to right, or right to left, up to down) all the letters of the alphabet.

Or

Play the game the same way only the pairs must leave the vowels off the chart, leaving blanks where the vowels should have gone. Or do the same, only place the vowels on the chart while leaving blanks for the missing consonants.

Scoring: The second team is timed after the first team has finished.

Easy

11. Noise

Setup: One player goes to the front with an opposing player.

Process: The first player is to recite the alphabet while the opposing player recites the alphabet incorrectly or backwards or randomly in order to confuse the first player. The second player cannot speak with more volume than the first player. The time of the first player is recorded, and the first player switches roles with the second player. The second player is timed.

Scoring: The shortest time to recite correctly the alphabet wins.

Moderate

12. Alphabet Race

Setup: One person from a team goes to the front. Emcee calls out any letter and starts the timing clock.

Process: The player must recite the alphabet starting on the called letter, going to Z, then starting the alphabet with A again, and ending at the letter that comes just before the first letter that started the race. The second team repeats beginning with a different letter.

Scoring: The team with the shortest time wins.

— Sam Sample, grade 11

19

Moderate

13. Alphabet Race II

Setup: Two people and a stopwatch
Process: The two people each race to complete the alphabet in the shortest amount of time with one of the stipulations below:

Only fricatives (f, v, s, z, etc.)
Only plosives (p, b, etc.)
No consonants
All consonants
Only consonants with two pronunciations (c, g, etc.)
Backwards
In its entirety

Scoring: Person to do it fastest wins.
— Jim Dolciamore, grade 12

Moderate

14. Alphabet Poem (Song)

Setup: Three teammates stand shoulder-to-shoulder facing the audience. They are given a topic, style, or tone to create with the task from the audience. This is a word-at-a-time game.
Process: One word at a time, beginning with an assigned letter, player one offers a word that begins with the assigned letter, and the second player continues that sentence with a word beginning with the next letter of the alphabet. The third continues with the next letter of the alphabet.

Example (starting with M):
A: (Sadly) **M**y
B: (Excitedly) **n**ote
C: (Angry) **o**pened
Etc.

The alphabet and the assigned tone or style control the creation of the group. The second team repeats the process with their assignments.

Scoring: Facilitator may consider using an audience blind ballot to determine the winner. Reproducible blind ballot cards are on pages 157-158.

— Stephanie Spock, grade 11

Phonics

Easy

15. Rhyme Race

Setup: Players are given a word or a syllable.
Process: Players have ten seconds (fifteen? twenty?) to offer as many rhyming (full rhyme? half rhyme?) words as possible.
Scoring: Whichever competitor offers the most correct responses wins.

Moderate

16. Rhyme Race II

Setup: Player is given a syllable (or a word).
Process: The player has thirty seconds to create a rhythmic poem in which the original word and full rhyme words end each line in the poem.
Scoring: It is judged on the number of full rhyme endings made; and for tie-breaking, judge the unity of the created poem.

Easy

17. Compound It!

Setup: Player is given a list of compound words and/or contractions on the board
Process: The player must pronounce them correctly. Repeat for second team's player.
Scoring: Highest number of correct pronunciations wins.

can't
we're
o'clock
he's
they'd

18. Sounds Like

Setup: Two players from a single team come to the front. The facilitator gets an idea for a scene from the audience.
Process: The two players do the scene speaking in gibberish. Each line must have a focus word or two where onomatopoeia clearly conveys to the other player and the audience the mimed or offered object. The second team has its chance at a sixty- to ninety-second scene.
Scoring: The team that has the best clarity of the onomatopoetics of the focus words is the winner.

19. Name That Sound

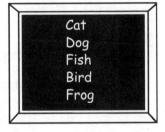

Cat
Dog
Fish
Bird
Frog

Setup: Player stands in front and a single syllable word is projected on the board and is not read aloud.
Process: The player must clearly pronounce the sound of the first, middle and last letters in order when prompted by the facilitator when the facilitator says, "First sound," "Second," etc.
Scoring: An elimination (spelling bee) format works best — if correctly done, the player goes to the end of the line to wait their turn to compete again. If incorrect, they must go to their seat. Last competitor standing wins.

20. Short or Long?

Setup: Player stands in front. Facilitator pronounces a single-syllable word

Example: bit, bite, tap, tape, not, note

Process: The player says either "short" or "long" based on

the sound of the vowel in the word. Five words per player.
Scoring: Highest score of correct answers wins.

 Easy

21. Family Reunion

Setup: Player is given a projected list of a word family. **Process:** Player must pronounce the words correctly. Repeat with a different list for the second competitor. **Scoring:** Highest number of correct pronunciations wins.

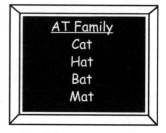

 Easy

22. Exceptions Aloud

Setup: Player is handed a set of cards (or a list) with irregular words. Reproducible cards with examples of irregular words are on pages 119-124.
Process: The player needs to pronounce them correctly.
Scoring: The player who correctly pronounces the most words on the list wins the round.

 Easy

23. Syllable Count

Setup: Player is given a word auditorially.
Process: Within five seconds she must give the correct number of syllables in the word.
Scoring: An elimination (spelling bee) format works best — if correctly done, the player goes to the end of the line to wait their turn to compete again. If incorrect, they must go to their seat. Last competitor standing wins for their team.

Easy

24. Keep 'Em Short

Setup: The focus is to get the competitors to say as many one (or two, or three, etc.) syllable words as possible in a short amount of time.

Process: One at a time, players go to the front and are given a limited number of seconds to say clearly as many words as possible with only the required number of syllables. Or, two players from opposing teams go to the front, and at the facilitator's signal alternate saying words with the correct number of syllables.

Scoring: The first to run out of words or make a mistake loses.

 Easy

25. New Words

Setup: Player stands in front of the audience. A new word from more complex word families, or that is regular and multi-syllabic, is written or projected on the board.

EI Family
Weigh
Neighbor
Receive
Receipt

Process: The player must decode and pronounce it correctly within a limited time set beforehand.

Scoring: An elimination (spelling bee) format works best — if correctly done within the time limit, the player goes to the end of the line to wait his turn to compete again. If not, he must go to his seat. Last competitor standing wins.

 Moderate

26. Syllable Scene

Setup: Two players from one team go to the front and are given a scene to play. Reproducible scene starters are on pages 151-156. The facilitator gives them a number (for example: one, two, or three).

Process: During the scene each line has to begin (or end) with a word that has that number of syllables.

Scoring: Points are given for errors or not talking to avoid errors. The players with the least points win for their team.

Moderate 🖉

27. Vowel Scene

Setup: Two players from one team go to the front and are given a scene to play.

Process: The first letter of the first word of each line must begin with the next vowel in the "a, e, i, o, u" sequence (The game can also be the Consonant Game doing the same thing with the consonant sequence).

For example with vowels:

Player A: **A**fter I swing, put the club away.

Player B: **E**xcellent idea. Thanks.

Player A: **I** thought so.

Player B: (Etc.)

For example with consonants:

Player A: **B**efore I do my homework, I have to go to the store.

Player B: **C**an I go with you?.

Player A: **D**on't know. Ask Mom.

Player B: (Etc.)

Scoring: First competitor to make a mistake loses. Or, an elimination (spelling bee) format works well — if correctly done, the player goes to the end of the line to wait their turn to compete again. If incorrect, they must go to their seat. Last competitor standing wins.

Moderate

28. Long and Short Race

Setup: One player goes to the front. The facilitator times the task.

Process: The player, going through the vowels in order, must speak two words for each vowel, the first word having a long version of the vowel (A) and the second having a short sound of that vowel. Do the next vowel (E), etc. The next team repeats the process.

For Example:
A: tray, ham
B: tree, sled

Scoring: The shortest time wins. (Maybe the only acceptable words fit within a category from a book being read, a civilization studied in another class, etc.)

Moderate

29. Endings Begin

Setup: One person from each team of five is on-stage at the same time.

Process: The facilitator flips a coin to see who goes first. The first person starts off by saying any word that he wants. After that the person from the opposing team has to say a word that starts with the same sound that the opponent's word ended with.

For Example:
A: Bellow
B: Oklahoma
A: Ugly
B: (etc.)

When someone makes a mistake or takes longer than the allotted time (five seconds?), that player is out. Another player from that same team replaces the errant player and has to make the correction immediately.

Scoring: The team with a player remaining on stage wins.

— Colin Brown, grade 12

30. Spot the Hidden Letter

Setup: Two players from opposing teams begin a scene. Reproducible scene starters are on pages 151-156.

Process: No player should use a word that has a silent letter in it. When one of the players says a word with a silent letter (the "e" in phone, or the "l" in should, etc.), he is penalized and a horn is honked by one of the judges. The second player, upon hearing the error/horn, shows the facilitator he knows that the other person made a mistake. This is done by starting the next sentence with the letter that wasn't heard (i.e. "Should we go?" is followed by "Later, perhaps." The missing letter is the "l" in should. The second player beginning the sentence with "l" shows he knows the "l" was left out).

Scoring: Person with the least errors wins.

— Jim Dolciamore, grade 12

31. Greater Than or Equal To

Setup: One player from each team comes on stage and performs a scene in which they have to include a pre-chosen phonetic sound in every spoken line.

Process: Now the catch: The number of assigned phonetic sounds has to grow with each sentence up to five, at which point the number recedes back to one.

For example: (both are to work with long "e" sound)

A: My tree! (One long "e" sound)

B: She killed my tree. (2)

A: He will ski to the nursery for a gardener. (3)

B: He will free my tree. Don't you see? (4)

A: I can't believe she would ski into my tree. (5)

B: Gee, I can see my tree is free now that it is hurt. (4)

A: Etc. (Back down to one long "e" sound.)

Scoring: Whichever team runs out of players first loses. Points would be based on a three-point system and awarded for vowel sound accuracy, creativity and pace.

— Bronson Vazquez, grade 12

Difficult

32. Dialects

Setup: The class is broken into two teams which take the stage on each side. The first three players from each team come to the front.

Process: These three people prepare to do a scene (Reproducible scene starters are on pages 151-156) where each vowel in every word (even silent vowels) is pronounced with their long sounds.

For example:

A: (At the store I bought milk.) Ate thee st-oh-r-ee I b-oh-ewe-ght m-eye-lk.

B: (Really.) R-ee-aye-ll-ee.

C: (I hate milk.) I ha-aye-t-ee m-eye-lk.

A: (etc.)

If any player makes a mistake, she drops to the wings and another player takes the out teammate's place exactly from the error.

Scoring: This is an elimination game. The team left with a player on stage alone wins.

— Jonathan Kenworthy, grade 11

Vocabulary

33. Finish Your Plate

Setup: Player is given a vocabulary list of words (two to ten).
Process: Players must use all the words correctly in one or more sentences. Difficulty goes up as all vocabulary words must be used in fewer sentences (and perhaps with performed punctuation done at the same time).
Scoring: An elimination (spelling bee) format works best — if correctly done, the player goes to the end of the line to wait their turn to compete again. If incorrect, they must go to their seat. Last competitor standing wins.

34. Beginnings and Endings

Setup: Player is given a set of cards with prefixes and suffixes to look at and show. Reproducible prefix and suffix cards are on pages 125-130. Facilitator may choose to make more.
Process: Player must pronounce the term and say the meaning of the term.
Scoring: An elimination (spelling bee) format works best — if correctly done, the player goes to the end of their team's line to wait their turn to compete again. If incorrect, they must go to their seat. Last competitor standing wins for their team.

35. Beginnings and Endings II

Setup: Two players have separate sets of cards, each with a random combination of prefixes and suffixes. Reproducible prefix and suffix cards are on pages 125-130. A scene idea is given to the pair by the audience.
Process: They are to play the scene. At the same time

each line spoken by each player must have a word that uses the pre- or suffix on the top of their stack. After using the top card's term in a line, the player then puts that card on the bottom of the stack; the next line spoken by that same person must use the next pre- or suffix. The scene goes for a limited time.

Scoring: The number of cards used correctly by the players is their score. The second team then performs with two new stacks to determine the winner.

Easy

36. Word Sort

Setup: Player or team is given a list of ten to fifteen words on the board.

Process: The player must sort them into categories (for greater difficulty, they may

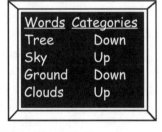

Words	Categories
Tree	Down
Sky	Up
Ground	Down
Clouds	Up

also discover the categories) within a time limit.

Scoring: The player or team that correctly sorts the grouping most quickly wins.

Easy

37. Morphing

Setup: Each team produces a two-person sub-team that competes. Facilitator puts three cards up in front that spell a word (i.e., "c/o/w"). Reproducible "ABC" cards are on pages 103-115.

Process: The two-person team is given the other twenty-three letters of the alphabet on similar cards. Within sixty seconds the team can add or delete any letters in order to create other real words (i.e., now, how, sow, low, etc.).

Scoring: The team that creates the most real words is the winner.

Easy

38. All Together Now! II

Setup: The audience or team determines the physical or vocal action for each of their vocabulary words that captures the essence of the word. For example, if one vocabulary word is "stretch," the group may agree that the action involves putting your arms up over your head, twisting your body, and yawning. All performers watch and memorize the actions for the vocabulary words as the facilitator and audience choose them. The actions/vocals are then reviewed by the facilitator and performers. Teams are made for the competition. Random sub-lists are made (for instance, if there are twenty vocabulary words with actions and four teams, then each sub-list for each team has five words from the master list).

 Easy

Process: One player does the actions determined by the audience, the team first confers and agrees on the vocabulary word and they all call it out (right or wrong). This continues until all five words are guessed. The second team goes.

Scoring: The team who says the words most quickly, wins. Penalty points for an incorrect guess.

39. Magnet Words

Happy
Tired
Sad
Energetic

Setup: Player is shown four words, two of which are antonyms and two of which are synonyms.

Process: The player must point out the correct pairs when asked to identify the antonyms and then the synonyms. Competitor competes with a new set of pairs.

Scoring: An elimination (spelling bee) format works best — if correctly done, the player goes to the end of the line to wait their turn to compete again. If incorrect, they must be seated. Last competitor standing wins.

40. Word Match

Setup: Ten words are on the board. Each team produces a player who, one at a time, competes.

Fish	Ferret
Frog	Frown
Fan	Fog
Fellow	Friend
Foe	Four

Process: Facilitator says aloud one of the words on the board. The player has a limited time to point to the correct written form of the word.

Scoring: Tally the number correct out of ten. Process repeats with the second team's player and a new set of words.

41. Mellow, Medium, Mad

Setup: Three players go on stage. The facilitator gives the team one card with three synonyms on it in order, top to bottom, set in a sequence of increasing (or decreasing) intensity (i.e., irritation, anger, rage).

Process: The three players have ten seconds to assign words to each other, agree on and set a location, and begin a scene. The players who are in the audience observe and can stop the scene any time within ninety seconds when they are ready to guess the word assignments. One audience player goes on stage (or directs the players verbally) to stand side by side onstage in the order (left to right) of increasing (or decreasing) intensity. At that point the team in the audience guesses the word assignments in the increasing order.

Scoring: Points are awarded for the correct intensity sequence order, and for guessing correctly the assigned word.

Moderate

42. Root Repeat

Setup: Three players from one team are chosen. Two go to the front and one leaves to avoid hearing. The players in front are given a card with several words which all share the same root (i.e., commune, communicate, excommunicate, communion, etc.).

Process: The two prepare a scene in which they can naturally use these words in context. The third player returns to observe the scene. The observing player must try to guess the root that keeps reappearing in the scene.

Scoring: There might be a limited number of guesses. Players can be penalized for over-pronouncing the words on the cards with the root. The second team gets a different root set on cards. The team that identifies the root most quickly wins.

Moderate

43. Homy-nuts

Setup: Two players take the stage. The homonyms in question are given. The facilitator, with the help of the audience, identifies distinctions between the words in question, and together they figure out a way to physicalize or vocalize the difference. (i.e., "Their" has an "i" in it and none of the other confused words [there, they're] do. One can emphasize the "i" by pointing to one's eye while saying the word. The word "they're" has a "y" in it, so a player using that word may have to put his/her hands in the air and sign when using that homonym. Another action would be established for "there.")

Process: The players have to do a ninety-second scene suggested by the audience correctly physicalizing each of the words in focus for the game.

Scoring: Points are scored with smooth use of the words in each line and accurate physicalization. Points are lost for inaccurate use and physicalization. One with most points wins.

Easy

44. The General's Ladder

Setup: The player is given a stack of cards that have a mixed order of levels of specificity.

Example: dog, mammal, animal, living things

Process: In a limited amount of time the player must put the cards in broadest (descending) or narrowest (ascending) order of specificity.
Scoring: The player with the fastest time wins.

Easy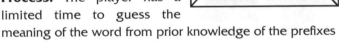

45. Fix This!

Setup: Player is given three to five words on the board that have prefixes and/or suffixes. The roots should be familiar to the performers.

rerun
monolog
analyze
kindness

Process: The player has a limited time to guess the meaning of the word from prior knowledge of the prefixes and suffixes.

Scoring: An elimination (spelling bee) format works best — if correctly done, the player goes to the end of the line to wait their turn to compete again. If incorrect, they must be seated. Last competitor standing wins.

Moderate

46. Liar's Club

Setup: Four players of one team go to the front and stand shoulder-to-shoulder facing the other team. Each is given a card with the same word printed; the word has a root, and a prefix and/or suffix. Each of the four cards has the dictionary definition of the word. One card, however, has a star (some marking) showing that this player is to use the real

35

definition. The others must make up reasonable definitions based on the word parts that are not the real definition.

Process: The facilitator pronounces the word to the opposing team who listens to the standing team players present their version of the word's meaning. They guess which definition is correct.

Scoring: Points go to the opposing team for correct guesses. Points go to the standing team for each guess that is incorrect. One with the most points wins.

Moderate ✏️

47. Homonee-Quips

(Note: This game can be played with any homonyms or words that need to be drilled into the players' heads.)

Setup: Two players take the stage and are given a set of words that are commonly confused (examples: there, their, they're). The facilitator then gives the two a scene they must play from an audience suggestion.

Process: Each player must talk until the words in question have been used. The second team is then allowed to offer two players to compete with new homonyms (examples: two, too, to).

Scoring: Members earn points by how many times the words/homonyms were used correctly in the scene.

Moderate ✏️

48. Sybil

Setup: Two players go to the front. The facilitator reads a word aloud that has multiple meanings (examples: wind, bill, club).

Process: One at a time the players offer one meaning in alternating order. If one runs out or goes blank, the other has a chance to offer another meaning. This goes on for two to four words.

Scoring: The player with the most meanings offered wins.

Moderate

49. Emotional Words

Setup: Four players from each team are on stage.

Process: Each player takes a turn saying a word that corresponds with an emotion word, and has to progress in the order of the alphabet. The player must express whatever emotion the specific word suggests.

Examples:
Person 1 says **a**ngry, while acting mad.
Person 2 says **b**ruise, while acting hurt.
Person 3 says **c**ry, while acting sad.
Person 4 says **d**ance, while acting happy.
They continue until they reach Z.

Scoring: The team that says all the words the fastest with the most correct words/emotions wins.

— Erin Justice, grade 12

Moderate

50. End-Rhyme Scene

Setup: Form two teams of three players each. One player from each team is center stage: The others are in the wings. The audience chooses the scene, characters, etc.

Process: One of the players starts the scene by saying a sentence. The other player says a line that has a word that rhymes with the last word the other player said, but it can't be the last word of the sentence.

Example:
A: My friend has a pet hog.
B: Pigs are gross! A dog is better.
A: I sent a letter to her about it. (etc.)

Scoring: If a player messes up, the player is out; replace with the next player from the same team. The team with one player left at the end wins.

— Brian Kelley, grade 10

Moderate

51. Voracious Vocabulary

Setup: One player from each team takes the stage. Each player is given five slips of paper. Each slip has an interesting or difficult (subject-appropriate) vocabulary word. The players are then given a scene to act out. Reproducible scene starters are on pages 151-156.

Process: Throughout the scene, the players must pull out a slip of paper with a vocabulary word and attempt to use it correctly in a sentence that fits the scene and its progression. Once a word has been introduced, either player can use that word over and over appropriately.

Scoring: A point is awarded every time a player correctly uses a vocabulary word in the scene. At the end of an allotted time, the scene is ended and points tallied.

— DJ Burk, grade 12

Easy

52. Vocabulary Relay

Setup: There are two teams of five. The facilitator writes down a sentence (on an overhead or blackboard), and then the other four teammates get into a line.

Process: The first person erases a word from the sentence and replaces it with a synonym. Next teammate steps up to the sentence and does his/her word replacement. Each person on the team does this until the 60-second time limit is up. Then the process repeats for the other team with a second sentence.

Scoring: The team with the most synonyms used wins.

— Tom Norman, grade 11

Parts of Speech

Easy

53. Point the Part

> The short cow smoothly jumped over the shining moon.

Setup: A player is either shown or told a short sentence. The facilitator identifies a part of speech (noun, verb, etc.).

Process: The player must identify each instance where that part of speech appears in the sentence offered. Or, player is given a noun (or two) and/or a verb (or two) and must use the words correctly in a sentence.

Scoring: An elimination (spelling bee) format works best — if correctly done, the player goes to the end of the line to wait their turn to compete again. If incorrect, they must be seated. Last competitor standing wins.

Moderate

54. Honk It!

Setup: One player goes to the front and stands in front of the other team. Before beginning, the player is given a structural item to use (e.g., prepositional phrases, appositives, clause types, etc.).

Process: The task is to tell the story enthusiastically while using the required item as often as possible, as naturally to the story as possible so that the listening team hears the story more than the required item. Whenever they hear the required structural item in a spoken sentence, they are to make a horn-honking sound.

Scoring: The listening team earn points for honking correctly; the performing player gets points for undetected usages. At the end of sixty to ninety seconds, the listening team produces a performer who narrates using another required element for the other team. The team with the most points wins.

Moderate

55. Honk

Setup: One player from each team goes to the front. Each has a horn in hand or has been given a sound or physical action to be performed every time the assigned part of speech is spoken in their two-person scene or conversation.
Process: The scene or topic for a conversation is assigned. Possibly the facilitator has chosen nouns as the focus. As the speaking unfolds every time a noun is said, the speaker (or the opponent) must honk (make a verbal sound or do the action assigned).
Scoring: It can focus on the number of correct honks, the number of errors, penalties for delaying the scene, etc. One with the most points wins.

Moderate

56. This Part Only!

Setup: The focus is to get the competitors to use as many of a certain type of speech (i.e., adjectives, nouns, abstract nouns, verbs, prepositions, etc.) as possible in a short amount of time.
Process: One at a time, players go to the front and are given a limited number of seconds to say clearly as many words as possible using the required part of speech. Or, two from opposing teams go to the front, and at the facilitator's signal alternate saying words that are the required part of speech.
Scoring: The first to run out of words or make a mistake loses.

Moderate

57. Dropout

Setup: Two players from opposing teams go to the front where the facilitator gives a scene to perform. Reproducible scene starters are on pages 151-156.
Process: In the sixty- to ninety-second scene the

competitors must speak all sentences with incorrect subject-verb agreement.

Examples:
A: They is going to the store.
B: Are I going with them?

Scoring: Correct agreement is counted as an error by the facilitator. One with fewest errors wins.

Moderate

58. Dropout II

Setup: Two competitors take the stage. The facilitator gets an idea for a scene from the audience. The facilitator identifies any grammatical rule that all players know (S-V agreement, consistent tense, complete thoughts, use of past participle [not the past tense form] with helping verb "to have," etc).

Process: The competitors must do a scene where each spoken line (can be more than one sentence) has to have the error version of the rule identified above (i.e., a sentence spoken must not agree in number between the subject and verb).

Scoring: Correctly using the grammatical rule identified is counted as an error by the facilitator. One with fewest errors wins.

Moderate

59. Switch

Setup: Two players from opposing teams go to the front where the facilitator gives a scene to perform. Reproducible scene starters are on pages 151-156. The facilitator at various points calls out "switch."

Process: To begin the scene, players must use sentences with perfect subject-verb agreement. At "switch" the players revert to incorrect agreement (similar to Drop

Out). This continues for the pre-determined scene length.
Scoring: The winner is determined by which player is able to correctly or incorrectly use subject/verb agreement depending on the time of the scene.

Moderate

60. Parts Expert

Setup: Two players go to the front. They are given a scene to play. Reproducible scene starters are on pages 151-156.
Process: Each player is given a part of speech that must be present in the line(s) before the partner can speak the next line.
Scoring: Points are scored by the number of lines spoken with the required part(s) of speech in a limited-time scene. The second team then takes its turn.

Moderate

61. Parts Idiot

Setup: Similar assessment vehicle as Parts Expert but this uses the opposite demonstration. Two players go to the front. They are given a scene to play. Reproducible scene starters are on pages 151-156.
Process: Each player is given a part of speech that must never be present in his/her line(s).
Scoring: Points are scored by the number of sentences spoken without the required part(s) of speech in a limited-time scene. The second team then takes its turn.

Moderate

62. To Be or Not to Be

Setup: Two players take the stage and are given an idea for a scene. Reproducible scene starters are on pages 151-156. The scene proceeds.
Process: Neither can use any form of the verb "to be." The facilitator honks a horn if the verb shows up. (Option: Set up the scene as indicated above, but require all sentences

to have a form of "to be.")

Example:
A: I want a lollipop.
B: Go get one.
A: I need money.
Etc.

Scoring: Player with fewest mistakes wins.

63. Tense Scene

Setup: An agreed upon number of players from one team go to the front. Each is assigned a verb tense, or all are given one tense. The facilitator gets an offer from the audience for the scene.
Process: The players do the scene within a time limit, and each must use only their assigned tense.

For example:
Player A (future): I am going to the store. Do you want to go?
Player B (past): No, I went yesterday.
Player C (present): That is too bad. Good-bye.
(Etc.)

Scoring: Points are scored by each player for use of their assigned tense and then the team's score is tallied. The team with the most points wins.

64. Scene without a Word

Setup: Two competitors take the stage and each (or both) is given a part of speech (or word).
Process: The competitor cannot use the part of speech or word in the scene. If it is used, a buzzer goes off.
Scoring: In the scene, the number of errors is counted.

65. Where to Begin

Setup: Two competitors take the stage and are given an idea for a scene. Reproducible scene starters are on pages 151-156. The facilitator has handed each a stack of cards with different parts of speech on them. Reproducible parts of speech cards are on pages 131-133.

Process: The scene proceeds as each competitor looks at the top card, shows the audience (somehow), and speaks a line that must begin with that part of speech. Then the other player speaks beginning his line with the part of speech from the top of their stack. The scene must end well with the last sentence from the last card (i.e., an exit, or the problem solved).

Scoring: Facilitator may consider using an audience blind ballot to determine the winner. Reproducible blind ballot cards are on page 157-158.

Moderate

66. Verb Wars

Setup: Two players from the same team are given a scene to play. Reproducible scene starters are on pages 151-156. One player is assigned to use only action verbs (i.e., sizzles, eats, stands), and the other only state-of-being or linking verbs (i.e., is, have, does).

Process: The scene is played for a pre-determined amount of time. The facilitator can call "Switch!" during the scene at which point the players must exchange their verb responsibilities.

Scoring: Points are either earned for acceptable sentences, or negative points for errors and delays that kill the pace of the scene. (Note: this game can be set up as a tie-breaker where errors cause the erring player to be booted and replaced by a player — see Scene Without ... page 50.)

Moderate

67. L.O.W.: Location, Occupation, Weapon

Setup: Two teams of three players compete. One team sets up by Player One staying and Players Two and Three leaving. The facilitator gets a Location, Occupation, Weapon from the audience. The location must include a preposition (on, under, in, etc.), the occupation must include an adjective (a blind janitor, a hyper lollipop inspector, etc.), and the weapon also must have an adjective (a wet feather, etc).

Process: The facilitator calls in Player Two. Player One tries to convey the "L" (location) to Player Two using only mime, gibberish, sound effects, and melodies (no lyrics unless they're gibberish versions). When Player Two thinks he has the location, Player Two nods and uses the acceptable techniques (mime, gibberish, etc.) to convey his own version of the location to check for accurate understanding. If Player Two has it, Player One moves to the "O" (occupation) with the same techniques. When done, they move to the "W" (weapon). When the weapon is conveyed, Player Two nods and Player One sits. Then Player Two calls in Player Three and the process repeats between Player Two and Player Three. When Player Three has the L, O, and W, Player Three nods and Player Two sits, and the facilitator asks Player Three for the L, the O, and the W.

Scoring: The descriptions MUST be exact and have the correct prepositions and adjectives. Total points possible are three (one each for L, O, and W). The second team then does its turn.

Moderate

68. Stand and Deliver

Setup: This is an "Empty Bucket" format game (The game is just a process for which you can require any particular grammar, punctuation, syntax element). This description will exemplify the ability to know and use adverbs correctly.

Process: One Player from a team goes to the front. The facilitator asks the audience for a topic about which the performer will present a ninety-second speech (or a product/service and the performer presents a commercial; or a two-person scene). The facilitator prepares the timer and a judge (one or two from both teams to ensure a correct assessment) to conduct the timing and to count the number of adverbs used in the presentation. At the end of the time limit, the number of correctly used adverbs (no repeats allowed) is decided, and the next team goes to the front and makes their effort to present more adverbs in the ninety-second time limit.

Scoring: Team with the most points wins.

69. Counting Clauses

Setup: Two competitors take the stage and are given an idea for a scene. Reproducible scene starters are on pages 151-156. The facilitator has handed each player a stack of cards with different numbers on them (one to five or greater). The scene begins.

Process: Each spoken sentence/line must have a number of clauses equal to the number on the top card of each competitor's stack. Dependent and independent clauses all count. Time limit.

Scoring: The competitor with the most points wins.

70. Have You Seen My Modifier?

Setup: Two players take the stage and are given an idea for a scene. Reproducible scene starters are on pages 151-156. The scene goes for a limited time.

Process: Each player must continue to speak until they have misplaced a modifier.

Scoring: The facilitator notes errors by honking a horn. Error frequency determines a winner and loser.

Moderate

71. Don't Get Tense

Setup: One player from each team goes to the front to do a scene offered from the audience. Also from the audience or facilitator, a verb tense is offered (i.e., present).

Process: Players have to do the scene with pace and natural dialog using only the assigned tense. Any errors and they get "honked" by a judge with a horn and have to correct the error immediately.

Scoring: The winner makes the fewest mistakes. Players can get negative points for not advancing the dialog.

Moderate

72. Tense Exchanges

Setup: Two players from opposing teams go to the front and are given a scene to play. Reproducible scene starters are on pages 151-156. Also, they are given three verb tenses to play in a certain rotating order (i.e., present, past, future, present, past, etc.).

Process: They are to play the scene and their lines/sentences must follow that order. One player can say two sentences in a line, but the sentences must still follow that tense rotation.

Scoring: Scoring can be done with negative points for violating the rotation.

Moderate

73. Alpha-Parts

Setup: Four players from each team are on stage.

Process: Each person takes a turn saying a word that is a certain part of speech. They have to progress in the order of the alphabet. They can all work with only one part of speech, or they might have to work with a rotating set of parts of speech (i.e., noun, verb, preposition, noun, verb, etc.)

Example:
Person 1 says Angry (adjective).
Person 2 says Bounce (verb).
Person 3 says Cat (noun).
Person says Decent (adjective).

Scoring: The team that says their words the fastest with the least errors wins.

— Erin Justice, grade 12

Moderate

74. Every Adjective

Setup: Have a hat or bowl with pieces of paper all with different categories of eras, events, styles, etc. Three players from one team go to the front and are assigned one each of the three types of nouns (person, place, or thing).

Process: One at a time in a cyclical rotation each says an adjective with the noun type that fits the assigned noun category and the selected era/event/styles (i.e., "lean cowboy," "dude ranch," or "double-barrel shotgun").

Scoring: There is a time limit and the number of correct responses is counted. The process repeats for a second team. The team with the most correct responses wins.

— Rachel Hill, grade 11

Easy

75. Parts of Speech Relay

Setup: There are two teams of five. The facilitator writes down a sentence (on an overhead so audience can see), and then the other four teammates get into a line. Each is assigned one of the parts of speech (noun, verb, adjective, etc.).

Process: In a cyclical rotation one team's players go to the

> The dog ~~ran~~
> quickly down the
> curvy road.
> The dog fled
> quickly down the
> curvy road.

sentence and replace (or add?) the parts of speech they have been assigned and replace them with other words in that category. Each player goes up and the sentence keeps evolving.

Scoring: In sixty seconds the team with the most correct words used in the revisions wins. Possibly, the team with the most unified sentence wins. Or, the team with the most descriptive or energetic sentence wins.

— Tom Norman, grade 11

Punctuation

Moderate

76. Scene with ... or Scene without ...

Setup: Two players from one team are given a scene to play. Reproducible scene starters are on pages 151-156.

Process: The controlling rule is that every sentence spoken (Scene with ...) has to have the game's required element (proper names, semi-colons, commas, items in a series, adverbs, etc.). If they are playing "Scene without ..." then no spoken line can have that identified element (Note: Pure mime scenes are disqualified, or scenes where players say so little because they are afraid to try lose by default-"It is better to have tried and screwed up, than to never have tried at all.")

Scoring: Many of these games can be formatted to play as elimination games. This is one. Each team puts three players onstage and in opposite wing areas. Each of those teams assigns its players a number: one, two, and three (four or more if you want). The number ones on each team come out and are given a scene to play and the game requirement (i.e., play a scene without periods, without capitals, with nouns modified by two adjectives, etc.). Scene begins and lines alternate. When one of the players makes a mistake, the facilitator honks a horn and calls, "Replace," and the erring player leaves. She is replaced by the next numbered player on her team who must do a new line correctly to move the scene along. Pauses earn a "Warning!" call from the judge, and either or both players can get replaced for killing the pace of the scene. Whichever team has a player still onstage when the other team's last player has been booted, is the winner.

77. Start and Stop

Setup: Two players from one team go to the front. The facilitator gives the setup for a scene. Reproducible scene starters are on pages 151-156. The facilitator determines the punctuation rules to be used in the scene (consider punctuation that creates pauses: end marks, commas, semi-colons, etc.).

Process: The two run the scene, and wherever a pausing punctuation mark comes in a sentence that is spoken, the speaking player must freeze for an agreed upon amount of time (i.e., periods get 1-2 seconds and commas get a sigh).

Scoring: Points are gained or lost by the number of correct usages and/or errors made. The second team then does its scene. Whichever team has the fewest mistakes wins.

78. Punctuate This

1. where is the family dog
2. oh no they left him behind
3. what will they do

Setup: Player stands in front and the facilitator visually gives five sentences on the board.

Process: The player must point out any or all of the following that are missing: capitals, periods, exclamation marks, or question marks.

Scoring: Points are awarded for correct identification. One with the most wins.

79. Punctuation Ballet

Setup: One player from a team goes to the front, and the facilitator, with suggestions from the audience, gives a set of movements that represent punctuation marks that will be used in a short narrative.

Process: The player practices the movements under the facilitator's direction to establish them in the player's mind. Option #1 — Sentences, which have been recorded on tape are played over the stereo system (possibly with a musical background). The player must punctuate the sentence with the correct movements as it is played. Or option #2 — Two players from one team go up. One is to dance the punctuation and the other is to make up the narrative. The punctuation marks in question are clarified and the movements are assigned. The story can only go sixty seconds. Or option #3 — Same formats as above, but this version has an attitude. The audience might pick a movie style (i.e., western, horror, cool detective, science fiction, romance, documentary on insects, etc.). In that case the punctuation movements (and sound effects) assigned by the audience must fit that genre, as the story must.

Scoring: (1) All the required punctuation marks must be used, and (2) points are scored by the number of punctuation marks required in the narration that are performed accurately by the player based on the option selected above.

Easy

80. Capital Idea!

Setup: Player is given a sentence on the board that requires capitals in various places and for various reasons.

susie q is one
of mary's best
friends at
summer camp

Process: The player must point out or capitalize all of the letters requiring it. The sentences for each competitor must have the same number of capitals required.

Scoring: The player that capitalizes most correctly is the winner.

Moderate

81. Punctuate Your Neighbor

Setup: Two players of one team go to the front and are given a scene to perform. Reproducible scene starters are on pages 151-156.

Process: As player "A" speaks, "B" must punctuate "A's" lines with correct, assigned sounds or movements. Lines and punctuation go back and forth.

Scoring: Points are given for correct "punctuation."

Easy

82. Comma Along with Me

Setup: Project a block template of a sentence on the board. One competitor is in front, and the second team's competitor is blindfolded.

> I used to live in Dallas Texas but now I live in Colorado Springs Colorado

Process: Have the first competitor point out where the commas go. Second player removes the blindfold and then tries the same with the same sentences.

Or

Setup: Several simple sentences are projected and one or more have items in a series.

> 1. I have a dog a cat and a bird.
> 2. You have been to New York Paris and London.

Process: The player is to point out where the commas go. NOTE: Be sure there is agreement about the use of a comma before the final "and" or "or."

Scoring: One point for each correct answer.

83. Quotes

Setup: A short section from a narrative is projected with unpunctuated quotes in it.

The wolf said to the pigs I'll huff and I'll puff and I'll blow your house down

Process: Player must point out where all the quotation marks, commas, periods, question marks, exclamation marks, colons, and semi-colons go. Second player repeats with a new passage.

Scoring: One with most correct answers wins.

84. Capital Flash

Setup: Player goes to the front. A sentence with capitals in it (proper nouns, words at the beginning of sentences and greetings, months and days of the week, and titles and initials of people) is read slowly aloud.

Process: The sentence is read again, slowly, and the player, holding a card in his/her hands that says "capital," lifts the card quickly each time a capital is required.

Scoring: Points for correct responses (and possibly a minus point for each missed).

85. Punctuation Spasm

Setup: Each team produces a player who goes to the front. A scene is given. Reproducible scene starters are on pages 151-156. Each player is given a punctuation mark to which they are sensitive, perhaps allergic. The allergic reactions for each of the marks are assigned by the audience. Perhaps a comma forces "A" to sing a note like an opera singer, and questions marks cause the other player to snort like a pig.

Process: As the scene unfolds, there are two performative options: either the players can play the scenes as if the allergic reactions were invisible to the performers, or they can "see" the reactions and must build them into the scene itself.

Scoring: Facilitator may consider using an audience blind ballot to determine the winner. Reproducible blind ballot cards are on pages 157-158.

Moderate

86. Punctuation Twister

Setup: One player goes to the front and stands by a floor game board with punctuation marks set twelve inches apart around the sheet. Slowly the facilitator reads a short paragraph or excerpt that uses punctuation. Directions for making the Punctuation Twister board are on page 137.

Process: As it is slowly read, the player must put either a hand or a foot on the gameboard punctuation mark when it is required by the text read (in this order: right hand, then left hand, right foot, then left foot, etc.).

Scoring: The facilitator looks for the right punctuation and the correct order (though the timing might be a bit behind the slowly reading facilitator's pace.).

Moderate

87. Flash Dance

Setup: Each team sends up two players to compete, one of whom is a player/speaker and the other is a flashcard player. The two players are given a scene to play in the center. Reproducible scene starters are on pages 151-156.

Process: Each of the "flashers" is to the side closest to her team member, and is standing by a small table with punctuation signs resting on top. Reproducible punctuation cards are on pages 134-136. As the scene is enacted, the flashers must punctuate the spoken sentences for their players only. Or, instead of using flash cards the punctuators can do an assigned movement and/or sound for the

punctuation when it needs to be in the spoken sentences.
Scoring: The facilitator can give points for correct punctuation and take away points for incorrect punctuation.

Moderate✎ ## 88. Comma, Period, Out

Setup: There is a narrator in front of the audience with four players standing to the side.

Process: The four players are assigned a punctuation mark (example: comma, period). The narrator gets a scene idea from the audience and begins a story using The Form (see Author's Note, page 9). When the narrator gets to a sentence that needs a punctuation mark, one of the four players does a sound and a movement to represent it, (whoever was assigned it). Whenever someone (one of the four people) misses a punctuation mark, he has to sit down.

Scoring: This is an elimination game. As each round ends, there is a winner. Or, the winners of each round can then compete in a final round to determine the champion.

— Derived from Story, Story, Out by Becky Oschner, grade 11

Moderate✎

89. Random Marks

Setup: Two players are on stage to do a physical scene.

Process: The two players have ten seconds to prepare for a scene based on an idea from the audience. Whenever a player ends his/her first line, it has to be a new punctuation mark (i.e., "Don't you hate beans?" "I absolutely despise them." "Then stop eating them!"). The players cannot use the same mark twice in a row.

Scoring: The longer they can go without pausing (five seconds with nothing to say) or repeating the same mark, the higher the scoring.

— Derived from Alphabet Scene by Jon Kenworthy, grade 10

Moderate

90. Voice-Over with Punctuation

Setup: Each team sends two actors to the stage (Actor A and B from each team). The A's stand center stage while the B's stand to the sides. The A actors are physical actors, and the B's are the voices: When A from one team hears his partner speak, A moves his mouth to try to match the words spoken and does the punctuation for his own voice. The A and B from the second team operate in the same coordinated fashion. The facilitator gets a scene offer from the audience. The physical actors set up the stage and begin. When each hears his "voice" off to the side, he moves his mouth and uses his body to play the scene.

Process: The "mouths" act realistically and seriously but do a crazy physical action at the punctuation. Or, the "mouths" and "voices" have to justify the punctuation spasms as the scene continues.

Scoring: Each couple gets points on how many sentences are punctuated correctly and/or are judged on how well they justify; or they are judged on how many errors.

— Derived from Voice-Over (aka Dubbing)
by Heather Sowers, grade 12

Moderate

91. Punctuation Inferno

Setup: Two players are standing onstage next to each other.

Process: One is narrating a story while the other punctuates it with dance moves. There is possibly jazz or other background music. The punctuator is keeping rhythm with the background music until punctuation is needed, and he bursts out his mad dance skills. Every punctuation mark is a different dance move. The moves must coordinate with the background music, which is decided on by the audience (i.e., country, metal, disco).

Scoring: An elimination format works best — if correctly done, the players wait their turn to compete again. If incorrect, they must go to their seats. Last competitors standing win.

— Mindy Datema, grade 11

Moderate

92. "Obsessionpux" (obsession-poo)

Setup: Two players are in a scene picked by the audience or facilitator. Reproducible scene starters are on pages 151-156. Once they get their locations, player "B" goes outside the room.

Process: The audience assigns player "A" a quirk or obsession (Loves to breathe deeply, fearful of shoes, etc.). Additionally, the audience gives the player a punctuation mark that causes the player to react (sneeze, blurt out the name of a kitchen utensil) that is inflamed when the player hears a sentence spoken needing that certain punctuation mark. Member "A" goes out and "B" returns to be given her own quirk, punctuation mark, and reaction. Both players are on-stage and the assigned scene plays. It is each player's objective to identify which part of punctuation the other has been given, and vice versa.

Scoring: The player who identifies the other's punctuation mark first wins.

> — Derived from Emotional Body Parts, Obsession, Party Quirks by Jason Thibodeaux, grade 12

Sentences

93. Name That Sentence

Setup: Player is given two likely or unlikely words (Perhaps one is a verb and the other a noun).

Process: The player must use the two words in a complete sentence. Or, in a restricted amount of time the player must make as many different sentences as possible with the two given words in the sentences (any conjugated verb form is acceptable — i.e., to be: am, are, were, etc.).

Scoring: An elimination (spelling bee) format works best — if correctly done, the player goes to the end of the line to wait their turn to compete again. If incorrect, they must be seated. Last competitor standing wins. In the case of having the players create multiple sentences, the player who makes the most wins.

94. Sentence Charade

Setup: A pair from one team competes.

Process: One acts out a simple action given by the facilitator (beforehand and therefore the physical performer is prepared), and the other player must describe the action in a sentence.

Scoring: A correct answer must be accurate, though perhaps not the exact wording the physical performer or the facilitator offered.

95. Four-Sentence Scene

Setup: One or more players from a team go to the front. The group is given a scene to play from the audience, but can only use four sentence types in the scene (declarative, interrogative, imperative, and exclamatory).

Process: The sentences have to be spoken in a certain order. Possibly there is a time limitation.

Scoring: The team that correctly uses the assigned sentence types in order within the time limitation is the winner. An audience blind ballot might be used for a tie breaker. Reproducible blind ballot cards are on pages 157-158.

Easy

96. Now I'm Done

Setup: Player is asked five questions.

Process: The player must answer all five questions with complete sentences. Opposing player does the same with different questions.

Scoring: Competitor with the most complete sentence answers wins.

Easy

97. Now I'm Done II

Setup: Two players are told to have a conversation.

Process: They can only speak with complete sentences.

Scoring: After thirty seconds, the player with the most complete sentences wins.

Easy

98. Half Thought/Whole Thought

Setup: The facilitator has lists of ten sentences and fragments. One list is read to one team (or player).

Process: Player(s) states either each item is a "whole thought" (complete sentence, 'good' sentence, etc.) or "half thought" (fragment, 'bad' sentence, etc.).

Scoring: Team with most correct responses wins.

99. Describe It!

Setup: Player is asked to think of a particular thing. (the focus might be "tree.")

Process: The player must describe it with as many descriptive words as possible, speaking in complete sentences, for fifteen seconds. Repeat for second player.

Scoring: Facilitator counts the number of words or descriptions. Competitor with most wins.

100. Name That Sentence II

Setup: Player stands in front and the facilitator reads five sentences.

Process: After each sentence the player identifies it either as a declarative, exclamatory, imperative or interrogative sentence.

Scoring: Points for correct responses. One with the most wins.

101. Junior Sentence Types

Setup: The focus is to get the competitors to say as many statement sentences, questions, or imperatives as possible in a short amount of time.

Process: The sentences spoken don't have to be related; the facilitator might require that they be.

Scoring: All sentences should be complete. (Another option for older players might be that all the sentences must be fragments; any complete sentences are incorrect.) The competitor that meets the requirements the most wins.

Easy

102. Jigsaw

Setup: Projected on the board is a list of four sentences on a single subject, but they are out of an obvious order; or all the sentences fit a single subject, except for one sentence that is off topic.

> And Mom makes pancakes. After I wake up, I brush my teeth. I don't like zebras.

Process: In the first case the player must give the more coherent order; in the second the player might simply identify the off topic sentence. For the second case, actual jigsaw pieces may be used to help the competitor visualize the correct answer. Reproducible jigsaw pieces in which three fit together and one does not are on pages 147-150.

Scoring: An elimination (spelling bee) format works best — if correctly done, the player goes to the end of the line to wait their turn to compete again. If incorrect, they must be seated. Last competitor standing wins.

 Moderate

103. Pyramid Story

Setup: Four players go to the front and stand facing front shoulder to shoulder. The team is given an event by the facilitator from the audience.

Process: Beginning on the team's right, moving left, and then returning one player at a time to the first player to speak, the team is to relate the event. #1 uses a simple sentence, #2 a compound, #3 a complex, #4 a compound-complex, #3 a complex again, #2 a compound, and finally #1 a simple sentence which ends the event.

Scoring: Points are given for correct type of sentence. One with most points wins.

Easy

104. Get Back in Line!

Setup: Player is shown a sentence on the board that has its word order somehow mixed up.

Mary had a lamb little whose fleece was snow as white.

Process: The player must point out the words that are out of place and speak the correct revision aloud. Another player repeats with a different sentence.

Scoring: An elimination (spelling bee) format works best — if correctly done, the player goes to the end of the line to wait their turn to compete again. If incorrect, they must be seated. Last competitor standing wins.

Moderate

105. Which Witch Is Which?

Setup: The game needs two players and two or more different noise-making tools. The task is to perform a scene where the clauses alternate between independent and dependent clauses.

Process: One player begins a scene with a dependent and then an independent clause. The second player responds with a dependent clause. The first player continues following #2 this time with an independent, then a dependent clause. They continue to alternate. Either player can say more than two clauses, but still must observe the alternating requirement. Repeat pattern until the scene ends or a time limit has been reached.

Scoring: Person with least number of errors wins.

— Jim Dolciamore, grade 12

Moderate

106. Sentence Rotations

Setup: Two players from opposite teams go to the front. They are given a scene to play. Player A is assigned questions and commands, and player B is assigned statements and exclamations.

Process: The players speak in turns. Player A first must ask a question, after which player B must make a statement. Player A must then say a command, then B must make an exclamation. At that point the rotation goes back to the beginning and repeats.

Scoring: One with fewest errors wins.

— Stacy Reger, grade 11

Reading Comprehension

Easy

107. Junior College Bowl

Setup: A short paragraph is read to one team (or a player of one team). Or, questions could be about a story read to the group earlier in the day, or yesterday.

Process: The following (types of) questions are asked: Who are the characters? What is the setting? What actions took place? What is the relationship between the two (or three) characters? What does "A" want? What emotion is she feeling? What condition (i.e., "cold") is he in?

Scoring: Two teams play and the most correct answers wins.

Moderate

108. What's the Form?

> Because Johnny has a lead foot, the police officer gave him a ticket.

Setup: Players from both competing teams go to the front. A short passage is projected for all to see.

Process: Player(s) as quickly as possible must identify the structural trait of the passage (e.g., compare and contrast, cause and effect, sequential or chronological order, proposition and support) either vocally or by lifting the appropriate card with all the options presented on them.

Scoring: Fastest time, or most correct responses wins.

Moderate

109. Do It!

Setup: A technical manual (or set of instructions) is given to two competing players.

Process: Each must read and perform accurately the instructions.

Scoring: The fastest wins.

Easy

110. Chores

Setup: One team at a time stands as a unit on stage.

Process: The facilitator gives the team a one-step written instruction. The team, as a whole, must complete the task in unison. The facilitator then gives the team a two-step written instruction to be performed in unison. Finally, the facilitator gives the team a three-step written instruction to be done in unison. Process repeats for the other team with different instructions.

Scoring: The team with the best overall accurate performance of the instructions wins.

Easy

111. Chores II

Setup: One team at a time stands as a unit on stage.

Process: The facilitator gives the team a three-step written instruction, and the team, as a whole, must complete the task in unison. The facilitator then gives the team a four-step written instruction to be performed in unison. Process repeats for the other team with different instructions.

Scoring: The team with the best overall accurate performance of the instructions wins.

Easy

112. What It Is!

Setup: Projected on the wall is a list with six items. Some are single letters, some single words, and others are one or two sentences.

Process: A player points to the example of either a "letter," "word," or "sentence" when the facilitator says "letter," "word," or "sentence."

Scoring: Highest number of correct answers between the two teams' players wins.

113. Why'd It Happen?

Setup: Two players stand in front of the audience. The facilitator reads a short paragraph from a narrative.

Process: When done, the facilitator asks for an inferred or unstated cause-and-effect from the text.

Scoring: The first to answer correctly earns a point. The one with the most points at the end of designated round wins. Or, an elimination (spelling bee) format works well — if correctly done, the player goes to the end of the line to wait their turn to compete again. If incorrect, they must be seated. Last competitor standing wins.

114. In Your Own Words

Setup: Player is read an excerpt from his grade level.

Process: The facilitator asks the player to paraphrase or interpret some element from the text: main point, speaker's attitude toward something in the text. Or, the facilitator asks the player to retell the content using their own words.

Scoring: Points are awarded for the number of specifics recounted from the original. (Memorized wording may count in younger grades, but may not count in higher grades.)

115. Speed Reader

> A girl named Sue had a sister named Sara. They were very close.

Setup: A short passage is given to two players and is projected for the audience's viewing. A limited time is given for preview.

Process: The facilitator asks questions that can be answered from the text.

Scoring: The first player to answer the questions correctly wins.

116. Speed Reader II

Setup: A short passage is given to two players and is projected for the audience's viewing. A limited time is given for preview.

Process: The facilitator asks questions about the text that the players answer by stating either "fact," "inference," or "not answered."

Scoring: The first player to answer the questions correctly wins.

117. Between the Lines

Setup: Two players are given a short passage of prose or poetry. They have five minutes to read it for inferences or connotation not directly stated in the text.

Process: Demonstration can go two ways (at least). One, the team can perform the narration or action of the text, communicating all the inferences in any way they see fit (i.e., realism isn't essential). Or, they could stand in front of the audience and just list the inferences/connotations they identified in the text. The process repeats for a second team.

Scoring: Points are awarded for the highest number of supportable inferences presented.

118. Story Structure

Setup: One or two players can do this at a time. A relatively short children's story is read.

Process: The player is asked to identify with specifics (names, places, etc.) the sections in the narrative (i.e., information from the exposition, the complication moment, where is the crisis, identify the moment of the climax, etc.).

Scoring: An elimination (spelling bee) format works best — if correctly done, the player goes to the end of the line to wait their turn to compete again. If incorrect, they must be seated. Last competitor standing wins.

Easy

119. Alitterhyme

Setup: A short poem is read aloud and/or shown.

Process: One player is asked to identify one or more pair of rhyming words. The player can also be asked to identify any alliteration.

> Roses are red.
> Violets are blue.
> You are my friend.
> I wrote this for you.

Scoring: An elimination (spelling bee) format works best — if correctly done, the player goes to the end of the line to wait their turn to compete again. If incorrect, they must be seated. Last competitor standing wins.

Easy

120. What's Missing?

Setup: A set of letters (correspondences) is projected one at a time. In each there is either an item missing, out of place (date, proper salutation, body, closing, and signature), or there is no error.

Process: The player reviews the projection and identifies the missing, misplaced, or correct qualities of the letter format.

Scoring: An elimination (spelling bee) format works best — if correctly done, the player goes to the end of the line to wait their turn to compete again. If incorrect, they must be seated. Last competitor standing wins.

Moderate

121. Human Sentences

Setup: One team goes to the front standing shoulder-to-shoulder facing the audience. The facilitator gives the team a sentence with grammar, punctuation, or vocabulary elements important to the coursework.

Process: The team has thirty seconds to prepare a performance of the sentence that physically or vocally represents as many aspects of the vocabulary, parts of speech, and punctuation (whatever) as possible. The essence of the concept is that each player presents/performs one word at a time. For example, the facilitator gives the sentence, "The dog ran fast." Player one says the word "the" while pulling up a chair and standing on it (shows that it has a capital letter), pointing directly and forcefully at the second player to speak (as an article showing that "the" is much more specific than the alternate article "a," and beginning it all with a huge inhale to show that it is the beginning of a complete thought that is to come). This might be balanced by the last player to speak exhaling overtly to show that the complete thought is over.

Scoring: The breath, the capital, and the pointing earn 3 points so far for this team. Punctuation can be performed in equally revealing ways and can earn points. The second through the fourth players do their thing. Each player is then asked to identify what and why she did what she did, and points are awarded and tallied.

Easy

122. Ears and Actions

Setup: One or more players go to the front (based on the number of parts possible in the text to be read). The facilitator reads a short passage.

Process: The player(s) must act out (actions and objects) the scene while it is being read.

Scoring: Facilitator scores the performance on the number of elements recreated from the text by the performers. The second team then repeats with another passage of equal length and complexity.

— Jessica Honea, grade 11

Easy

123. Rumor

Setup: The entire team (4 - 6) is on stage. Each player has a piece of paper and a pencil.

Process: The facilitator hands a sentence on paper to Player One who reads the sentence to himself. He then writes his own version of the sentence on his piece of paper. Player One then shows Player Two his paper. Player Two then writes her own version of the sentence and shows it to Player Three. This continues until the last player has written her version of the sentence. The last player reads the revised sentence out loud, after which the facilitator reads the original sentence out loud. The process repeats for the second team.

Scoring: The way to judge which team wins is to see which final sentence is closest to the meaning of the original sentence.

— Erin Justice, grade 12

Moderate

124. Difficult Duos

Setup: Two players are given a short scene from a "difficult" writer such as Shakespeare. They are then given five minutes to review the short scene.

Process: After five minutes, they must perform their own version of the scene. Process repeats for a second team.

Scoring: Facilitator may consider using an audience blind ballot to determine the winner. Reproducible blind ballot cards are on pages 157-158.

— DJ Burk, grade 12

Storytelling

Moderate

125. Para-linz

Setup: Two players from one team go to the front. The facilitator gives the details for a scene. Reproducible scene starters are on pages 151-156.

Process: The scene must go sixty to ninety seconds, and each player must speak using parallelism in each line before the other player can speak again. Team two plays.

Example:
A: This mighty force, this power, you have, this strength controls you.
B: No, the calm, the wind, the silence is my master.

Scoring: Facilitator may consider using an audience blind ballot to determine the winner. Reproducible blind ballot card are on pages 157-158.

Moderate

126. Form It

Setup: Four players go to the front. Each is assigned a section of The Form (see Author's Note on page 9).

Process: The players have ninety seconds to tell a story with a good platform in the routine, elements of which are reincorporated throughout the rest of the narrative. Or, at more advanced grade levels the team might be required to present the fictional world of the story in a certain genre or story style consistently throughout the four storytellers. Or, each of the four storytellers has his own style in which to continue the story (#1 is children's story, #2 is horror, etc.).

Scoring: Facilitator may consider using an audience blind ballot to determine the winner. Reproducible blind ballot card are on pages 157-158.

127. Speeds

Setup: Two players from the same team (or competitively from opposite teams) go up front. The facilitator assigns the specifics for a scene (Who, Where, When, Why, and What). Reproducible scene starters are on pages 151-156.
Process: In this scene, which is to go from sixty to ninety seconds, the players must use sentences in the present, past, and future tenses that are justified. When the sentences are in the present tense, they speak and act in a realistic speed; when in past tense, speak and act in fast speed; and in future tense, slow motion speaking and movement.
Scoring: Facilitator judges on accuracy, use of all three, frequency of tense use, playing the scene well and with good concentration.

128. Yours and Mime

Setup: Two players from the same team go to the front. One is the narrator and the other is the mime.
Process: The pair is given a scene with a character (or more) to tell and act out. Reproducible scene starters are on pages 151-156. The task is for the narrator to tell the story in sixty to ninety seconds using as much concrete detail as possible. The mime is to physicalize and/or vocalize each concrete detail as it is given by the teammate narrator.
Scoring: Points are scored by the narrator speaking a concrete sensory detail AND the mime physicalizing it or reacting to it physically or vocally. The second team completes its version of a different scene. The team with the most points wins.

Moderate

129. I Know What You Meant

Setup: Two players take the stage and are given an idea for a scene from the audience. The scene proceeds. At any time the facilitator can honk a horn, or call "monolog."

Process: The speaking player finishes her line and freezes at which point the second player faces the audience and does what is essentially an unspoken thought sequence about what the other player really meant in her last spoken line. That monolog/interpretation is then built into the scene somehow. These scenes may go longer than ninety seconds.

Scoring: Facilitator may consider using an audience blind ballot to determine the winner. Reproducible blind ballot cards are on pages 157-158.

Easy

130. My Life

Setup: Both teams are given the instructions to prepare the acting of a short story that is from one player's life experience. The facilitator will give the instructions that the story is to be either "funny," "scary," "embarrassing" or "exciting" so that the story is to present an emotional quality.

Process: The team's story is to have a beginning, middle, and end according to the instruction and modeling in prior instruction. Facilitator may require that The Form (see Author's Note, page 9) elements be included. The preparation time is limited (i.e., three minutes). The facilitator flips a coin to determine which team goes first and second.

Scoring: The facilitator bases scoring on standards for narrative, focus, clear speaking, emotional tone, logic of order, and/or use of characters and setting.

Easy

131. Show Me More!

Setup: One player at a time stands in front of the audience. The facilitator reads a two-sentence event ("The boy ran. He fell.").

Process: The player then has ten to fifteen seconds to speak a revision of the offering that is much more descriptive. Each descriptive addition earns a point ("The tall boy ran quickly down a steep hill." = five points for "tall," "quickly," "down," "steep," and "hill."). The second player has a turn with a different set of sentences.

Scoring: The player with the most points wins.

Easy

132. Truth or Fiction?

Setup: Player is told to tell either "fiction," or "autobiography," or "explanation."

Process: For thirty seconds the player is either to make up a story or recount a true event in his life, or explain how to do an activity or describe a thing or player.

Scoring: Points can either be awarded by the number of sentences or the number of descriptive words or phrases.

Moderate

133. Getting a Rise

Setup: One player goes to the front for a sixty- to ninety-second story. Before starting the player is given a card with an effect to be achieved in the audience (i.e., to like the hero, hate the villain, tension, etc.).

Process: The storyteller tells a story that is to have an ending within the time period. At the end, the audience offers differing effects concerning the characters and the response to the events or descriptions.

Scoring: Points are awarded for each response from the audience that reflects the desired effect. Player with the most points wins.

134. Voices

Setup: Two players take the stage and are given an idea for a scene either from the audience or from the facilitator. Reproducible scene starters are on pages 151-156. The scene proceeds.

Process: The facilitator has assigned some combination of required voices from the two players: one must speak only with passive voice while the other must speak only in active; both speak in one voice only; both are assigned only one, but then the facilitator can call, "switch."

Scoring: Facilitator may consider using an audience blind ballot to determine the winner. Reproducible blind ballot cards are on pages 157-158.

135. Speech Spasm

Setup: One player goes to the front at a podium that has a covered flip pad. When the pad is flipped, the audience sees a surface that states an organizational pattern (i.e., comparison and contrast, topical categories, spatial, increasing importance, time, climactic order, etc.).

Process: The facilitator gets a subject from the audience, and the speaker has fifteen seconds to makes notes. The speech is to go a maximum of two to three minutes. Facilitator flips the first card and both the speaker and the audience see the first organizational pattern the speaker is to use. Once this pattern is being used in the speech, the facilitator honks a horn or a buzzer, and the speaker must continue, but flip the next card revealing a different organization which the speaker must immediately begin employing in the speech. The buzzer continues periodically. With twenty seconds remaining, the facilitator informs the speaker, "twenty seconds," and the speaker must conclude before the maximum time expires.

Scoring: Evaluation is based on the accuracy of each pattern required.

Moderate

136. Story, Story, Out (Prose Styles)

Setup: Four players take the stage shoulder-to-shoulder facing the audience. The facilitator sits downstage of the team in a closed position. Each player is given a prose category (e.g., short story, novel, essay, product instructions, etc.). An idea for a story is taken from the audience.

Process: When the facilitator points to a player, that player must tell or continue the story from the last speaker, only in her assigned style. If playing with "Out," when an error in continuity is made by a speaking player or by a player to whom the facilitator points, the erring player is out and must sit.

Examples:

Category	Styles
Dramatic Literature	Comedy, Tragedy, Drama
Dramatic Monolog	Human vs. Human
Conflict	Human vs. Nature,
	Human vs. Society,
	Human vs. Self
TV Show	News Report, Commercial,
	Soap Opera, Situation Comedy,
	Documentary
Movie	Romance, Teen Comedy,
	High Comedy, Horror,
	Science Fiction, "B" movie,
	3-D movie
Emotion	Happy, Depressed, Fearful

Scoring: The team with players standing the longest wins.

Moderate

137. Story, Story, Out (Audience Styles)

Setup: Four players take the stage shoulder-to-shoulder facing the audience. The facilitator sits downstage of the team in a closed position. Each player is given an audience to address in style, tone and content (i.e., three year olds, CEOs of a Fortune 500 company). An idea for a story is taken from the audience.

Process: When the facilitator points to a player, that player must tell or continue the story from the last speaker, only in his assigned audience. If playing with "Out," when an error in continuity is made by a speaking player or by a player to whom the facilitator points, the erring player is out and must sit.

Scoring: The team with players standing the longest wins.

Moderate

138. Story, Story, Out (Point of View)

Setup: A team of three stands on-stage shoulder-to-shoulder facing the audience. Each is given a separate point of view (first player, third limited, or omniscient). The facilitator gets a title or character or theme from the audience. The facilitator sits downstage of the trio and points to one player at a time.

Process: When pointed to, each player tells the story using their assigned point of view. When the facilitator switches pointing, the previous speaker stops immediately (mid-word, mid-sentence, etc.) and the new speaker must pick up the story/sentence exactly at the cut-off point, only with the new point of view.

Scoring: Judges score on the accuracy of the point-of-view work on the team and the quality of the narration.

Moderate

139. Give Me Your Tone!

Setup: Player is given a subject and an attitude with which the speaker of a speech or narrative is to talk (i.e., hostility, admiration, fear, etc.).

Process: The player is to speak for sixty seconds using a voice, body language, and vocabulary (tone) that convey the assigned attitude.

Scoring: Points are earned for the number of items that convey the attitude.

Moderate

140. Order in the Court!

Setup: Player goes to the front. Facilitator gives a topic about which the speaker must extemporaneously speak for at least sixty seconds. Or a story idea can be offered by the audience.

Process: According to the instruction given in the class, the player is to present a speech that has a beginning, middle, and end; the speech must also have concrete details. Or, if the audience has offered a story idea, the player has sixty seconds to tell a story that adheres to the structural elements taught.

Scoring: Evaluation is done by a rubric established during instruction.

Moderate

141. What Are You After?

Setup: Player from one team goes to the front and is given a communication to make (thank you note, love letter, book report, etc.) and an objective or purpose for giving the message.

Process: The random assignments might have the player speaking while pursuing a complimentary tone (i.e., love letter seeks the reader's amorous response); however, they might be "writing" a thank you note with a purpose of having the audience hate dogs, or hate the writer, etc.

Scoring: At the end of the allotted time, the team guesses the speaker's purpose (that must never be overtly stated during the performance), and if correct, they get a point.

Moderate

142. Down to Earth Narrative

Setup: One player from each team goes to the front and faces the audience.

Process: "A" has to tell a "tell" story in the most uninteresting abstract sentences, one sentence at a time. After each sentence "B" has to convert the abstract sentence to a "show" sentence with vivid details and sensory language.

For example:

Player A: Day began.

Player B: As the four boy scouts wriggled in their brown and green official scout sleeping bags under the canopy of tall redwoods, light shafts broke through the forest ...

At the end of ninety seconds, the roles reverse as the "A" player tries to score. Or, the game is essentially the same only the sequence is reversed. The first player speaks a wonderfully detailed sentence which the second player must reduce to a "tell" sentence, or a generality.

Scoring: Facilitator may consider using an audience blind ballot to determine the winner. Reproducible blind ballot card are on pages 157-158.

(NOTE: English teachers know it's better to "show" in writing, rather than "tell.")

143. Adverts

Setup: Two players from one team go to the front and are handed two to three cards with persuasive techniques (ethical or not) and a product or service to promote. The cards are shown to the audience.

Process: The players have ten seconds to confer, and then they must present a commercial to promote/sell the item assigned using the techniques given on the cards.

Scoring: Evaluation is based on the number of times the techniques were used in the time allotted. Repeat for the second team.

144. Speak!

Setup: Player goes to the front, is given a topic, and has thirty seconds to prepare the focus, structure, and position on the subject.

Process: The speech is given a limited and pre-arranged amount of time to be complete. A second player repeats the activity with a second topic.

Scoring: Evaluation is based on a pre-arranged rubric.

145. Bad Ad

Setup: One player goes on-stage and is given a product or service to promote/sell.

Process: The player has thirty seconds to fully stage a commercial that is filled with inadequate and inappropriate evidence promoting the product/service. The second team's player repeats the process with a different product.

Scoring: Points are scored for the concentration, conviction and production details along with the lack of quality argument content. Or, facilitator may consider using an audience blind ballot to determine the winner. Reproducible blind ballot card are on pages 157-158.

Moderate

146. First Line, Last Line

Setup: Two players from one team go to the front and are given a first and totally unrelated last line.

Process: The players must begin a scene with the first line and take the scene to the last line given so that the scene makes sense. Before beginning, the facilitator gives a scene requirement (i.e., every third line must be an exclamation, no commas, etc.).

Scoring: Points are earned by the least set of violations and by believable sequence of lines getting from the first to the last.

Moderate

147. Not Quite Scene

Setup: Two players take the stage. A player from the audience with a story ("Who here had an embarrassing date sometime?") is solicited to come on stage. That audience player is given a pair of different sounding buzzers: one sound means what was done on-stage is what occurred on the player's date; the other buzzer means the players' offer wasn't accurate.

Process: The two players must make offers trying to find/guess an accurate description of what happened to the audience player.

Scoring: Points are scored on quickness of the players' alternatives and the thoroughness of the scene (details and continuity) as they seek the player's experience through trial and error.

> — (aka 'Family Dinner' or 'ding-buzz') by Laura Livingston, Michael Durkin, Bay Area Theatresports™

Moderate

148. First Line, Last Line — Dropouts

Setup: Two to three players (or so) from each team. Two teams compete.

Process: The audience gives them a location. They act it out with bad grammar. Correct grammar is an error and eliminates the on-stage player, who is replaced by a teammate.

Scoring: Whichever team has a player on-stage last wins.

— Derived from First Line, Last Line by Sarah Bush, grade 10

Moderate

149. Turret Trade-Off or Spastic Story Time

Setup: Two players are standing.

Process: The players must improv a story by telling it in an alternating fashion: They trade off narration after any punctuation. Instead of saying or ignoring the punctuation, the player must do a movement and/or a sound for each individual form of punctuation. They must follow The Form format (see Author's Note on page 9).

Scoring: It can be scored on a scale from one to three on punctuation accuracy, following story line and The Form, creativity and pace.

— Bronson Vazquez, grade 11

Writing and Editing

150. What's the Point?

Setup: Two players go to the front. The facilitator reads a short expository paragraph.
Process: On paper the players write down what they believe the main idea of the text to be.
Scoring: Points are given for correct answers.

151. Write Right!

Setup: With a writing staff (solid upper and lower lines, with a dotted middle line) on the board, one player is given orally a simple sentence.

Process: The player must write the sentence on the staff with correct case sizes, spaces, and ending punctuation. All sentences used in a round should have the same number of letters, spaces, and punctuation required.
Scoring: Evaluation is based on the number of items done correctly.

152. Paragraphic

Setup: Two players go to the front. Each is given a topic sentence for a paragraph they are to write. (This game can be set up and begun while another competition is done in the interim.)
Process: Each retreats with paper and pencil to write the body of the paragraph using "simple supporting facts and details" to complete a unified paragraph. After the limited

time is over, each paragraph is read aloud.

Scoring: Evaluation is based on the number of supporting facts and details. (The truth of the facts is not important in that the players may not have equal background on the subject).

Moderate

153. Edit It!

Setup: Two competing players are given the same text that has some areas where editing would improve the coherence, progression, grammar, or punctuation.

Process: A limited amount of time is given for the revision notes. Perhaps the competitors do the revisions on overheads or on computers, some medium so that the revisions can be shown to the audience and facilitator.

Scoring: The one who most correctly edits the excerpt wins. If both competitors have equal points, fastest wins.

Difficult

154. Predict the End

Setup: Players both go to the front, and each is given a copy of a short story that neither has read. The final few pages of the story have been removed.

Process: Each is told to predict the end of the text. A limited amount of time is given for reading the responses. Both predictions are read aloud.

Scoring: Points are given for correct predictions and the use of specifics (names of characters, places, times, etc.).

Difficult

155. Sumo Sentences

Setup: Each team produces a player who comes to the front and stands by the Doneygraph (see Vocabulary, page 173) on the floor containing six essential words found on a sentence on the board (i.e., "Before the poet attempts to develop a sympathy in the reader for the protagonist, he sets the background of a normal, pleasant summer in the southern half of the nation.") The six bold items are examples of the words

Sympathy	Reader	Protagonist
Poet	Summer	South

found on the sections of the Doneygraph (see below).

Process: Two players from opposite teams stand on opposite sides of the graph on the floor like Sumo wrestlers. One is cued by the facilitator to begin and he grunts and stamps a foot on one of the squares on the graph. At that "cue" the second player must revise the sentence on the board beginning with the elements "stomped" by the cued player.

Scoring: If the judge accepts the revision as including all the essential elements from the original, a point is earned. If not, the stomping player gets a point. At that point the one who just revised stomps on another square, and another revision form must be made by the first stomper. This continues until all squares have been "stomped."

Moderate

156. Transition Position

Setup: Four players stand in front shoulder-to-shoulder facing the audience. The audience gives them a topic or a story idea to develop for 60 to 120 seconds.

Process: Each player, one at a time, offers a sentence to develop the story. The pattern starts on the left and moves to the right one player at a time. When the player on the right ends her sentence, the turn loops back to the player on the left and the pattern continues. Each subsequent sentence should follow from the content of the previous sentence (logical sequence). Beyond the general sense of flow, each player's sentence, beginning with the second player, should somehow have a transitional word or phrase at the beginning of the sentence that connects with the previous sentence (i.e., however, furthermore, and with this in mind, nonetheless, having forgotten what he just promised himself, etc.).

Example:
(Offering soda as a substitute for milk in the cafeteria.)
A: However, milk has nutrients soda does not.
B: Nonetheless, students prefer soda over milk. (etc.)

Scoring: The facilitator scores the transitions (or lack of) during the exposition or narration and determines the winner accordingly.
— Joe Bell, grade 9

Moderate

157. Sentence Scramble

Setup: One team is given a scrambled sentence such as "pickles I eat like to."
Process: They must unscramble it as fast as possible. Or, one team is given a sentence and must, using the same words, rewrite the sentence to show the same meaning but in a different way.

For example:
"He runs diligently" can be changed to "Diligently he runs."

Scoring: Fastest team wins.
— Samantha Sample, grade 11

Difficult

158. Thesis Thought

Setup: One player from each team takes the stage. They are given a set-up for a scene. Reproducible scene starters are on pages 151-156.

Process: They must attempt to conduct the scene using only thesis-type sentences throughout the scene.

For Example:

(Two men at a street-side cafe, drinking lattes)

Player A: Shakespeare was a brilliant playwright who used minor characters as foils to illustrate the flaws within his main characters.

Player B: People today lack the education and sensitivity to literary nuance in great literature due to the influence of television. (Sips coffee.)

Player A: (etc.)

Scoring: The player who used the most thesis-like sentences wins.

— DJ Burk, grade 12

Moderate

159. Active Anachronisms

Setup: Four players: two upstage will be a "scene"; two downstage do a "scene."

Process: First the two upstage players begin a scene using only active voice in the spoken lines. After four lines are spoken, they freeze. The downstage players begin the same scene using only passive voice.

Scoring: Facilitator may consider using an audience blind ballot to determine the winner. Reproducible blind ballot cards are on pages 157-158.

— Jim Dolciamore, grade 12

Difficult

160. A Positive Amendment

Setup: Two players from the first team take the stage. They are given a situation to act out. Reproducible scene starters are on pages 151-156.

Process: Every time a player mentions a proper noun, the other player must interrupt and tack on an appositive. They play for sixty to ninety seconds, then the second team repeats with a new situation.

Scoring: Winners use more appositives correctly within the time limit.

— DJ Burk, grade 12

More Language Arts Games

161. Point the Plurals

Setup: Player views a projected sentence on the board.

Many women are afraid of mice.

Process: She must point to and pronounce all the plurals in the sentence. Competitors do the same with another sentence.

Scoring: An elimination (spelling bee) format works best — if correctly done, the player goes to the end of the line to wait their turn to compete again. If incorrect, they must be seated. Last competitor standing wins.

Easy

162. Find It Fast!

Setup: One player from each team goes up. In front of each is an identical set of books.

Process: The facilitator asks a question that requires the player(s) to choose the correct title, go to the table of contents to find where to go in the book, and go to the correct chapter to give the required information that answers the question.

Scoring: First player to give the correct answer wins each round. Team with most points at end of game wins.

Easy

163. Dictionary Race

Setup: Two players go to the front, each with a dictionary.

Process: The facilitator gives the unknown word and asks for a specific piece of information from the dictionary (i.e., plural or singular? Earlier meaning? Second definition? etc.)

Scoring: First with correct answer wins.

Moderate

164. Scavenger Hunt

Setup: Two competing players go to the front. Each is given the same documents (almanac, newspaper, magazines, etc.).

Process: The facilitator asks for information contained within one of the documents. The two players race to offer the correct answer by "reading" the structural guideposts to get to the text with the correct answer.

Scoring: First to answer wins.

Easy

165. Forms and Features

Setup: Player goes to the front. On the board several items are projected one at a time. The items are either poetry, drama, fiction, or nonfiction.

Process: The player must identify the type of literature each is.

Scoring: Points for correct answers. The second player uses different projections.

Moderate

166. I Hear …

Old King Cole
Was a merry old soul.
And a merry old soul was he.

Setup: Player in front is told to listen for one or more of the following in a poem or prose piece to be read aloud and possibly projected on the board: rhymes, repeated sounds, instances of onomatopoeia.

Process: Player is to identify as many as possible. The second player is shown a second poem that has roughly the same number of items to identify.

Scoring: An elimination (spelling bee) format works best — if correctly done, the player goes to the end of the line to wait their turn to compete again. If incorrect, they must be seated. Last competitor standing wins.

Easy

167. Vocabulary Ladder

Setup: One player goes to the front. The player is given a vocabulary word.

Process: The player says the word, spells it, then picks a word from memory that begins with the second letter of the vocabulary word and spells that word. Then the player picks a word that begins with the third letter of the first vocabulary word and spells it. This continues until every letter of the primary word has been used to start another word.

For example:
Primary word given: Riot
Player: "Riot, R, I, O, T."
Continues   "Irate, I, R, A, T, E"
Continues   "Obvious, O, B, V, I, O, U, S"
Continues   "Team, T, E, A, M"

Scoring: Time how long the whole process took. A player from the second team repeats the process with a new word with the same number of letters. The shortest time taken determines the winner.

Moderate

168. Flip

Setup: Player goes to the front.

Process: Facilitator offers one word at a time and the player must give an acceptable antonym.

Scoring: An elimination (spelling bee) format works best — if correctly done, the player goes to the end of the line to wait their turn to compete again. If incorrect, they must be seated. Last competitor standing wins.

169. Flip II

Setup: Players from each team go to the front. The facilitator gives them a location or situation for a two-person scene. Reproducible scene starters are on pages 151-156.

Process: The players are to speak one sentence at a time. In the first line spoken there must be a word used that can have a reasonable antonym. The second player must incorporate into his line the antonym that is the "flip"/opposite from the first, while offering words that also can have a reasonable antonym.

For example:

Player A   Here we are in front of this tall building.

Player B   I'm a little short on cash. Can we climb up in the morning?

Player A   Nighttime is the only time it's open.

Player B   The sign says, "Closed."
Player A   Etc.

Scoring: Speed and accuracy earn points. Slowing the scene's pace earns penalty points.

170. Figure It Out!

Setup: In either spoken or visual form the player is offered some form of figurative language.

Process: They must accurately identify the type (e.g., simile, metaphor, hyperbole, personification).

Scoring: Most correct answers wins.

Moderate

171. Contraction Action

Setup: A player comes to the front and is either asked questions or must speak for thirty seconds.

Process: During that time every sentence spoken is to have at least one contraction (won't, can't, etc.).

Examples:
Sentence with two contractions:
You shouldn't sign up for a marathon if you can't go the distance.
Sentence with three contractions:
I haven't ever eaten seafood, I can't eat nuts, and I shouldn't eat desserts.

(Or, two players are to do a two-person scene alternating lines. Players must speak until they have used a contraction.)

Scoring: Points for contractions used and extra points for sentences with more than one contraction. Penalty points for sentences without contractions. Second player performs. The player with the most points wins.

Moderate

172. Figures of Speech

Setup: Two players from the same team are given a sixty-second scene to do. Reproducible scene starters are on pages151-156.

Process: Each spoken line (not each sentence) must have a figure of speech in it before the next player can speak a line. The object is to get more figures of speech in the scene in the sixty-second period. The second team competes with a different scene.

Scoring: Team with most figures of speech used in their scene wins.

173. Figure This

Setup: Two players from one team take the stage as the facilitator gives them an offer from the audience to control their scene. On either side of the stage is an assistant, each holding a stack of cards with a random order of the following terms: idiom, analogy, metaphor, and simile.
Process: The players have to justify body positions between open and profile so they can see the cards on one side of the stage or the other. Whichever way it makes sense for each to face (left or right), the flip card held and rotated by the assistants governs what figure of speech each must use with each spoken line in the scene. The acting team can face opposite directions; they can also face the same.
Scoring: Facilitator may consider using an audience blind ballot to determine the winner. Reproducible blind ballot cards are on pages 157-158.

174. Literalists

Setup: Two players take the stage and are given an idea for a scene. Reproducible scene starters are on pages 151-156.
Process: Each player must use metaphors and similes in her lines. Each figure of speech, however, must be taken literally and the literal offer must be incorporated into the scene.
Scoring: Facilitator may consider using an audience blind ballot to determine the winner. Reproducible blind ballot cards are on pages 157-158.

Difficult

175. Point of View

(Note: This game relies on the players being very comfortable with The Form, platforming, and reincorporation.)

Setup: Three players from one team approach the stage. The facilitator gets a location, event, or an object from the audience.

Process: The players assume three separate positions on the stage that distinguish one from the other. If lights are available, the players have moved to spiked locations so that each operates in a tight light. In this case the light operator randomly brings up one spot at a time, possibly for a pre-arranged time length. Fades can occur during a sentence or at some nice "end-able" moment in the monolog. To begin, one player "comes to life" and begins talking either in the context of the audience's offer, or about the item offered. Either by the player's choice or the light operator's, that monolog ends, and one of the remaining players begins another angle on the event or character offered in the first monolog (another point of view). When that second speech is done, the final character comes to life and adds a third and final point of view from another character (or time) that is to provide a sense of closure to the three-scene account. Then the second team has an opportunity to perform.

Scoring: Facilitator may consider using an audience blind ballot to determine the winner. Reproducible blind ballot cards are on pages 157-158.

Difficult

176. RatioMinute
(Parallel relationships in a minute)

Setup: One player from a team is the charade mime.

Process: The player gets a list with ten items, each of which completes an SAT-like metaphor (People: boy :: Books: _____ [phone book]). Basic charades. Just before each new item on the list is attempted, the facilitator reads the relationship sentence.

Scoring: The remaining players have one chance/guess to get it right. If correct, they get a point. Second team repeats the process. Team with the most points at the end wins.

Moderate

177. Spelled Out

Setup: Three players take the stage and are given a scene suggestion. The audience then picks out a letter for the focus of the game.

Process: Throughout the course of the scene, the player must spell out any word(s) that begins with the focus letter (i.e., If the letter were "s," this might be one line: "I s-a-w a young girl wearing a s-m-o-c-k."). Or, this game could be revised to do the same basic process with any part of speech.

Scoring: Points are given for the number of correctly spelled words, or negative points for missing the words to be spelled, or misspelling words.

— DJ Burk, grade 12

Moderate

178. Obsession

Setup: Two to four players in a scene. Setup doesn't matter much. One player is a host (optional).

Process: Each player has an obsession with grammar, punctuation, or form. One obsession could be with capital letters. Another with questions. Another with simple sentences, etc. The host has to find out what their "punctuation quirk" is.

Scoring: Whoever messes up the least and sticks with their quirks wins.

> — Derived from Obsessions/Party Quirks by Levi O'Loughlin, grade 11

Difficult

179. Poets' Slaves

Setup: Each team offers a team of four members to do a scene. Reproducible scene starters are on pages 151-156.

Process: Starts out with a normal improvised duet poem, but with two teams, with player one from team one giving a line, then player one from team two giving a rhyming line. The difference? While one person is giving a line, the other is doing punctuation performance — (the vocal and physical spasms with the punctuation marks). They continue doing this back and forth until one player from one of the teams either takes too long rhyming (predetermine a time limit), or responds too late with a spasm. If either messes up, then that person goes off-stage and is replaced immediately with another player from their team.

Scoring: Errors are counted against each team. When one team runs out of players, the other team wins.

> — Derived from Duet Poems by Shannon Roybal, grade 11

Game
Supplements

Several of the game descriptions in *Grammar Wars* require the use of flash cards or game pieces. For your convenience the following reproducible items are included and pages noted with the games that require them.

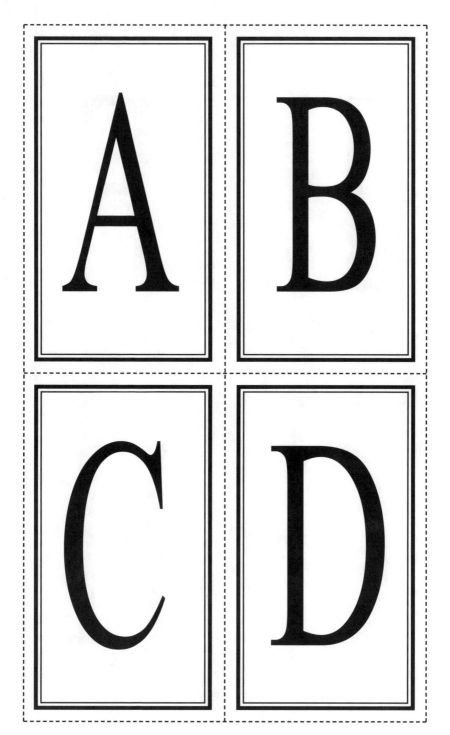

E

F

G

H

104

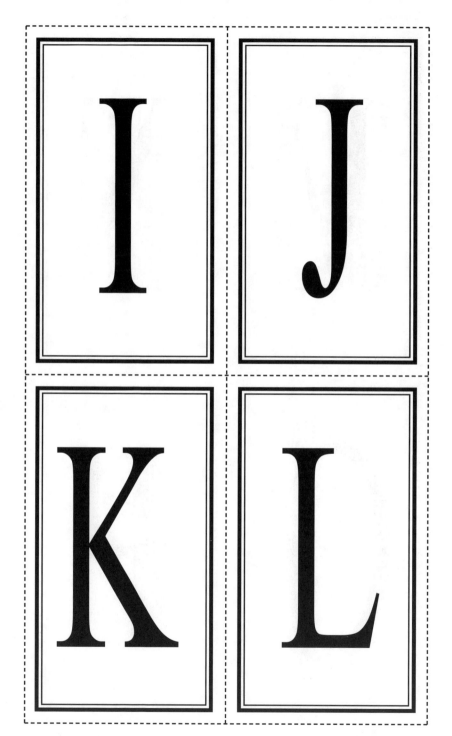

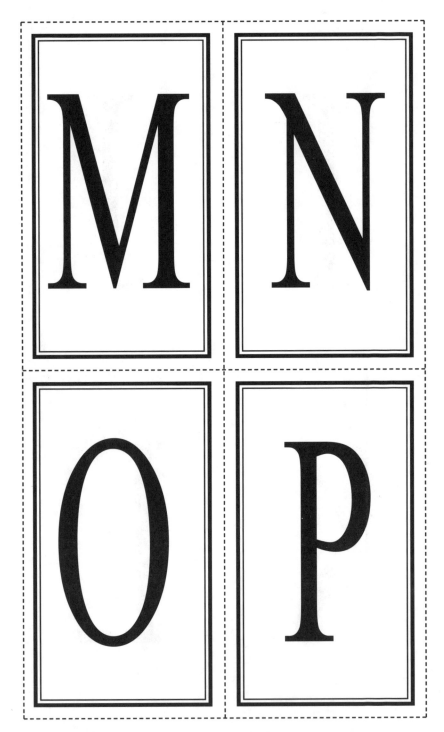

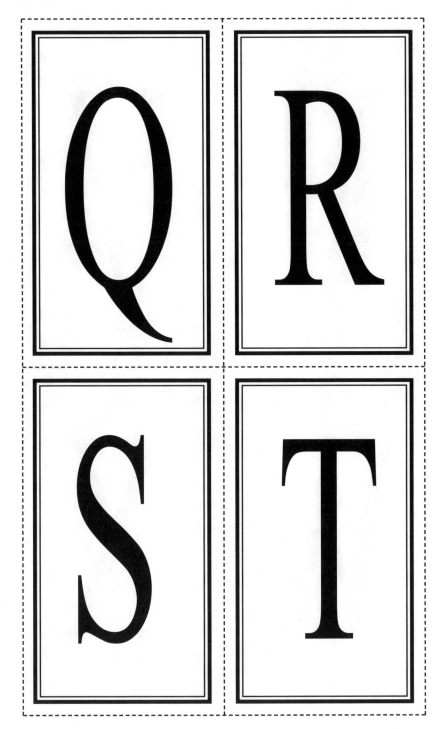

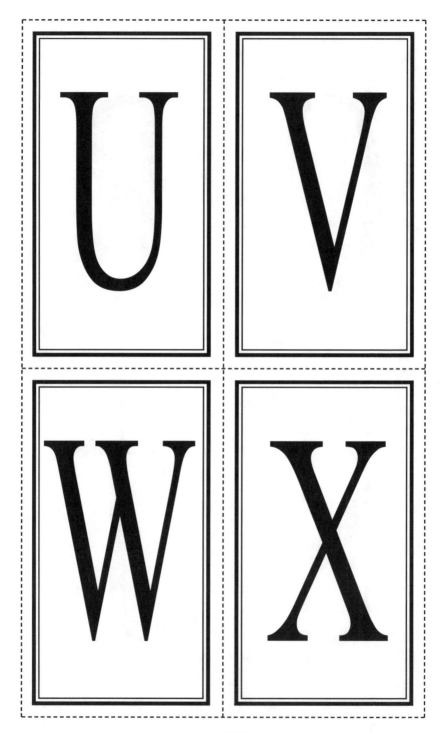

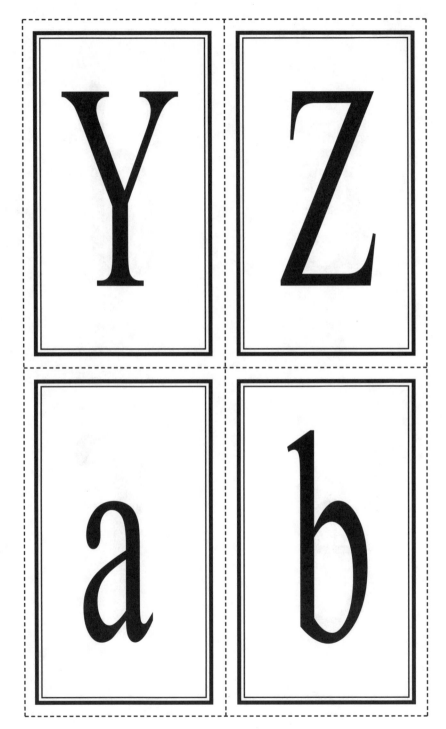

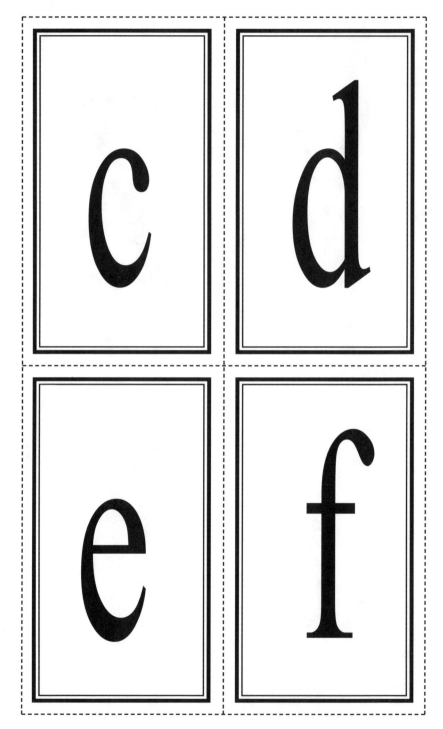

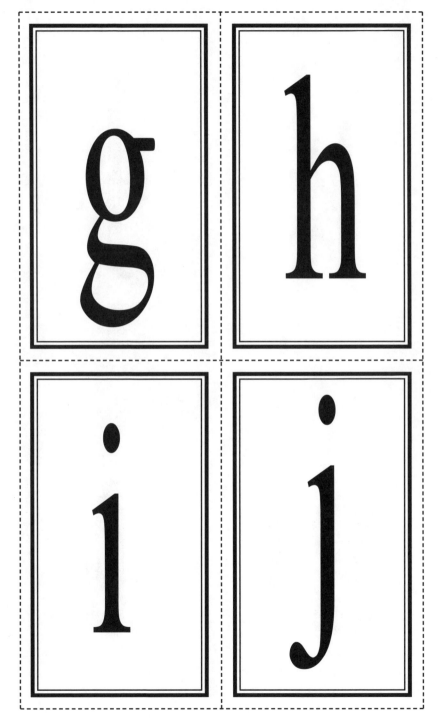

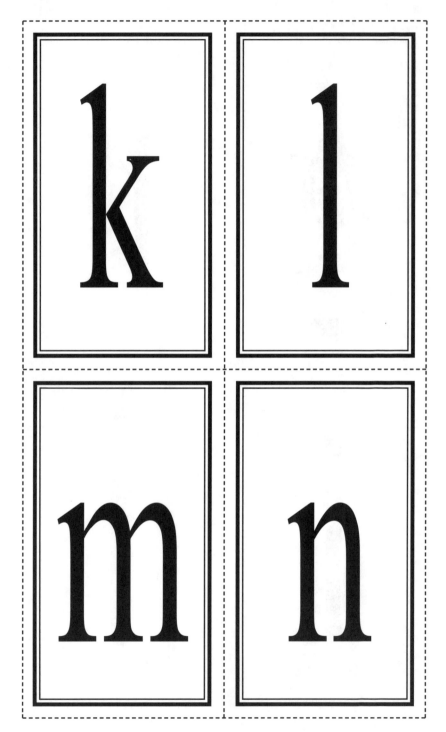

k l

m n

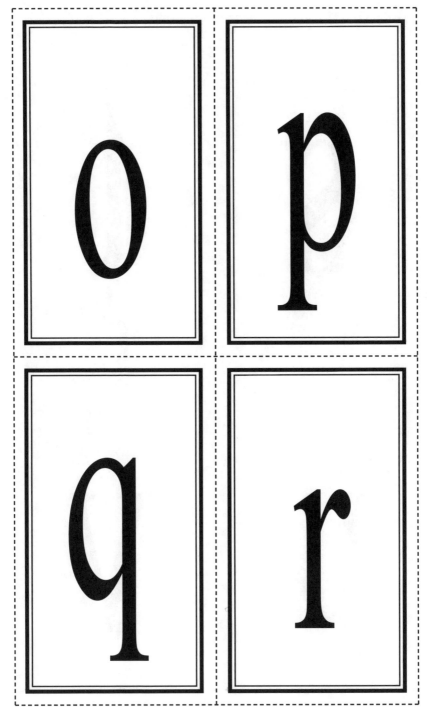

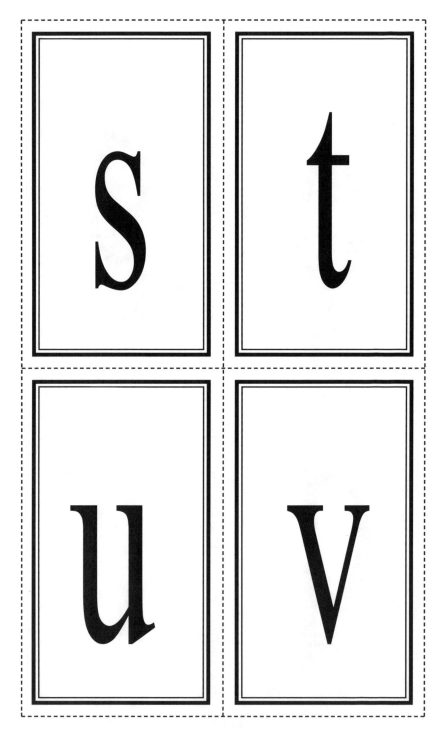

s t
u v

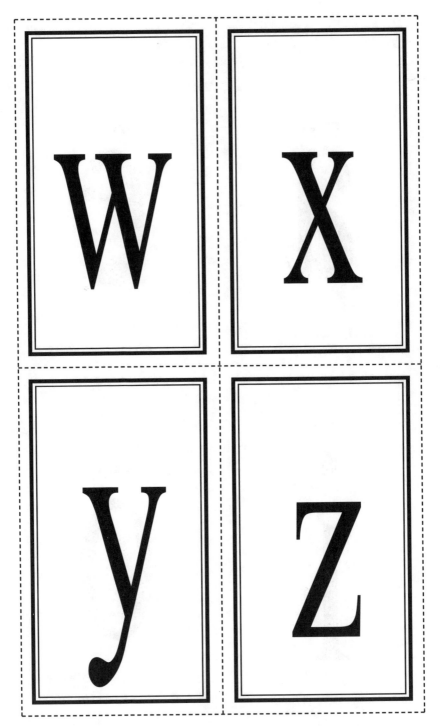

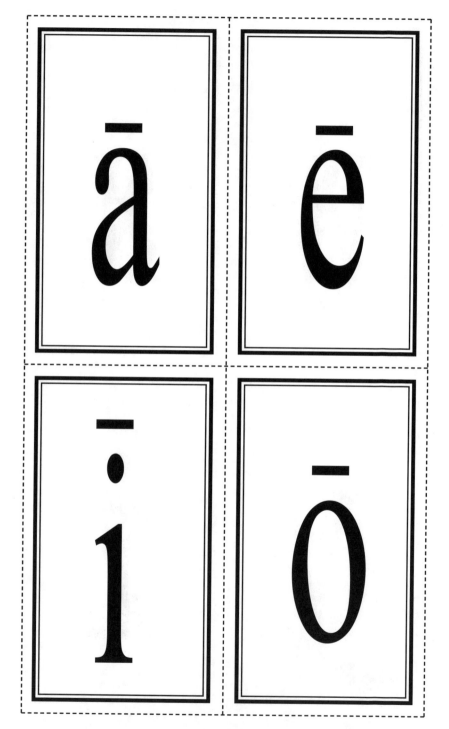

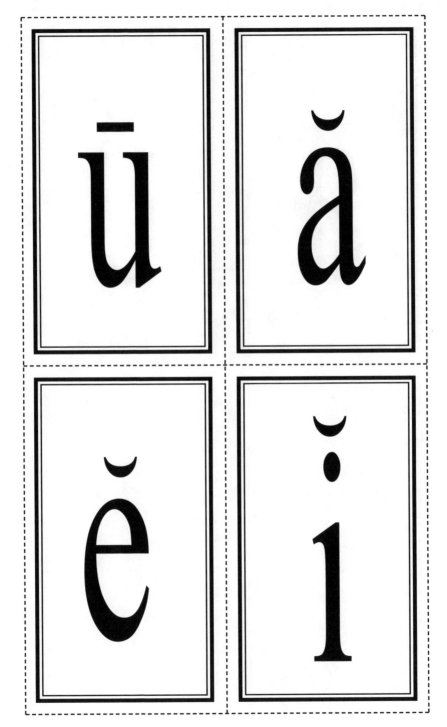

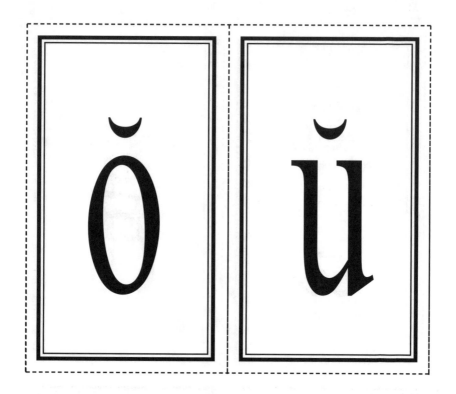

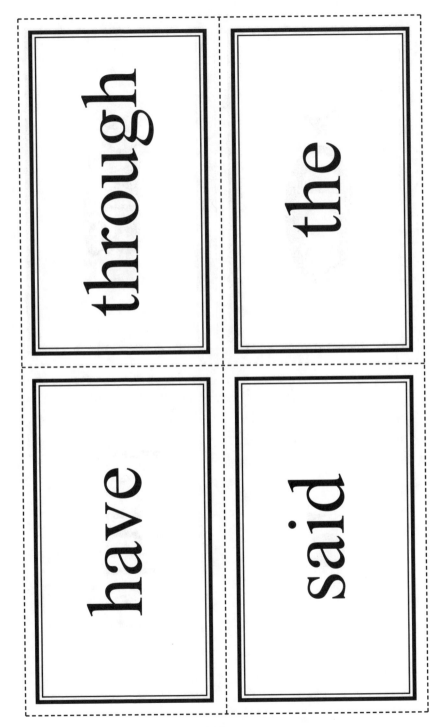

through

the

have

said

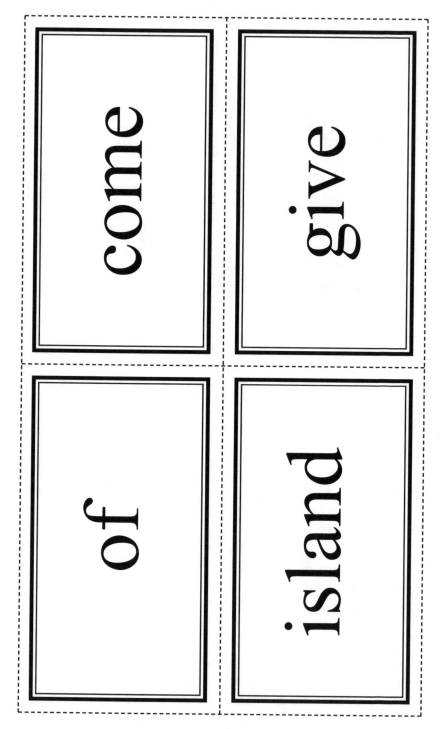

come

give

of

island

went

action

weigh

rhythm

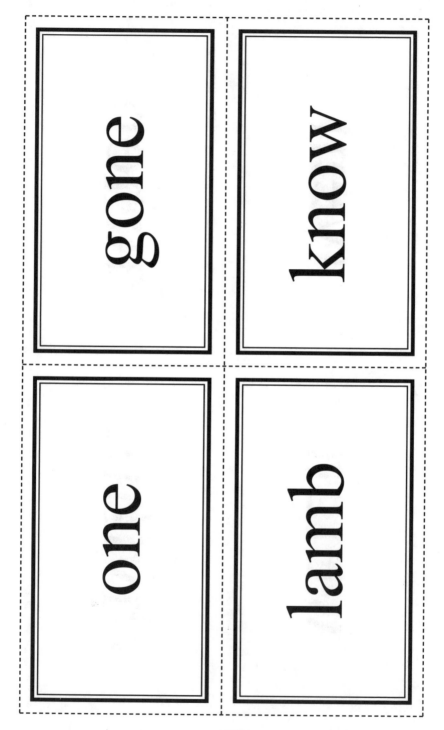

gone

know

one

lamb

been

other

comb

boat

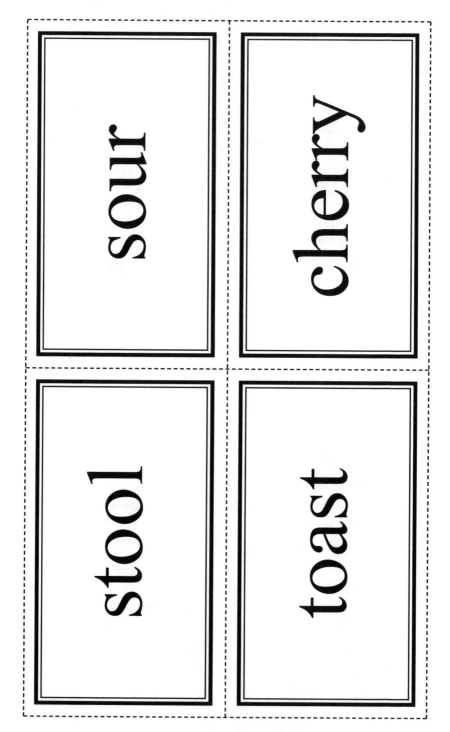

sour

cherry

stool

toast

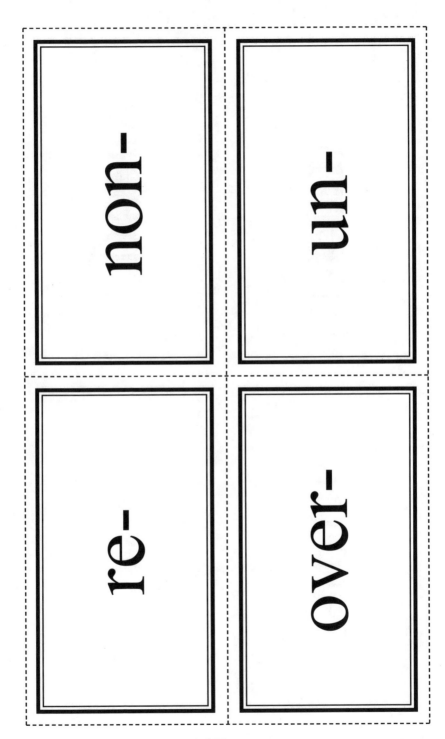

non-

un-

re-

over-

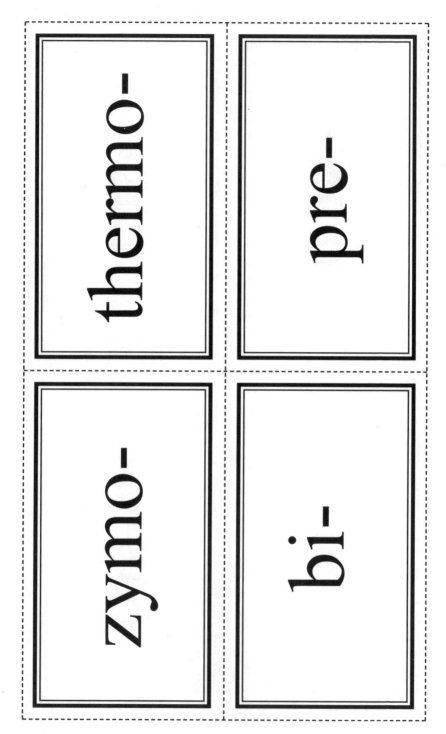

thermo-

pre-

zymo-

bi-

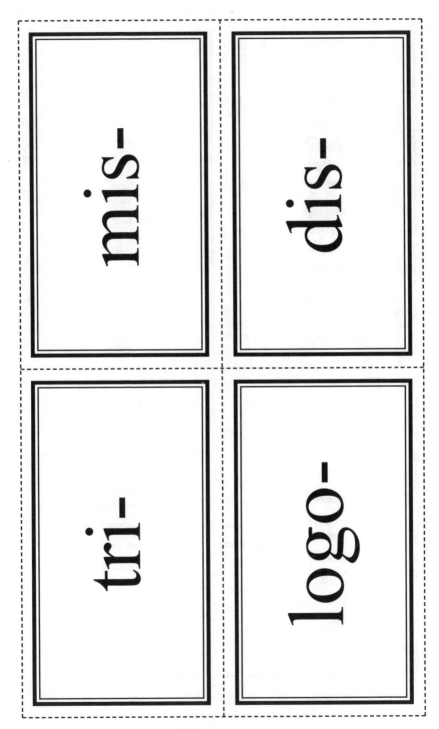

mis-

dis-

tri-

logo-

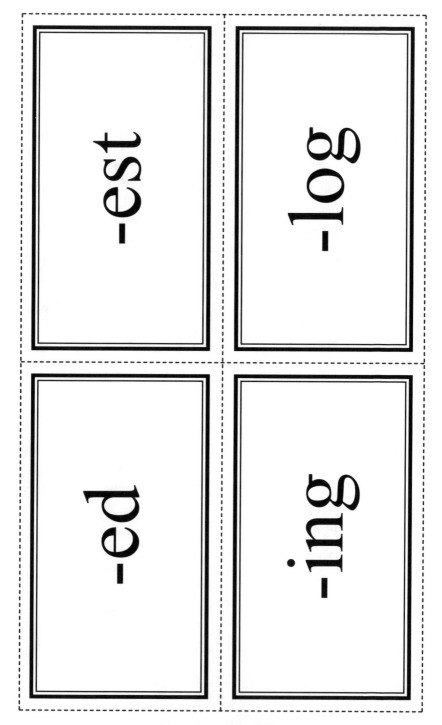

-est

-log

-ed

-ing

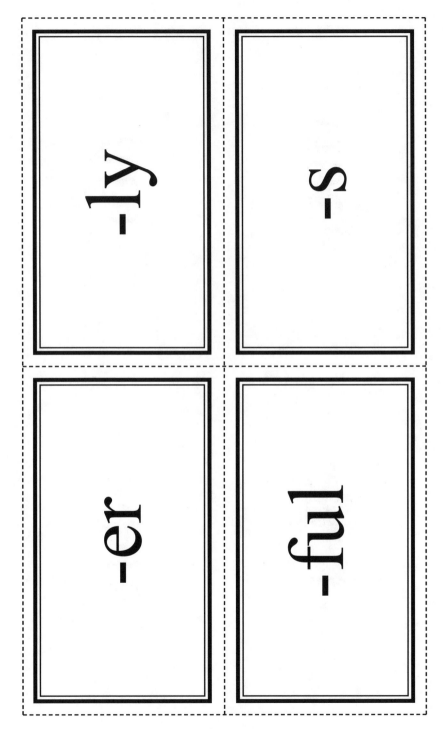

-ly

-s

-er

-ful

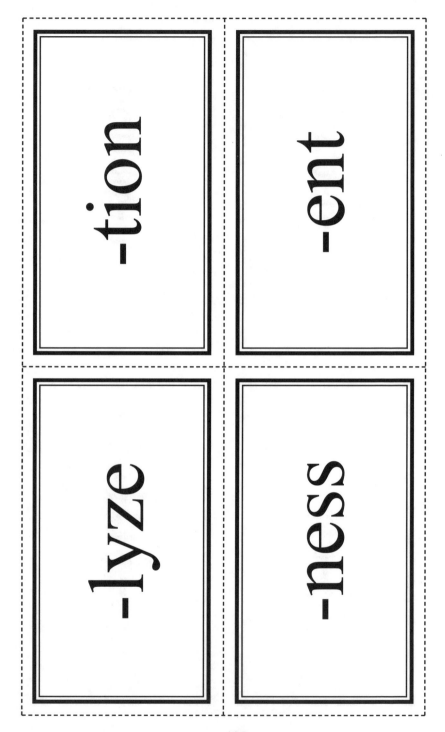

-tion

-ent

-lyze

-ness

demonstrative

conjunction

article

interjection

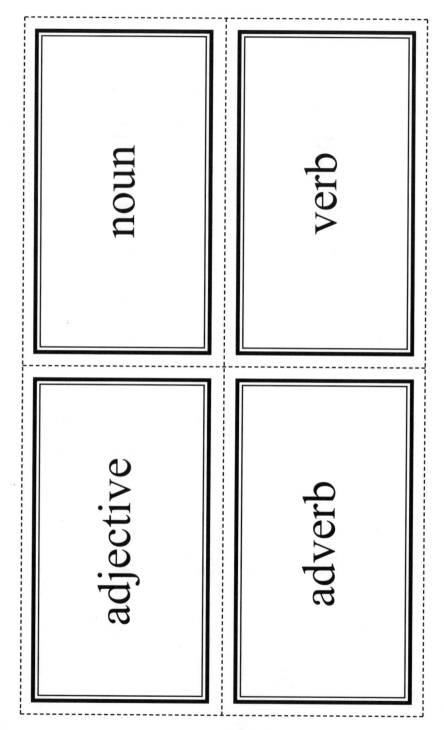

noun

verb

adjective

adverb

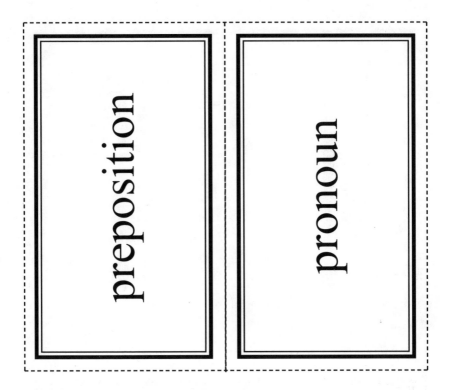

preposition

pronoun

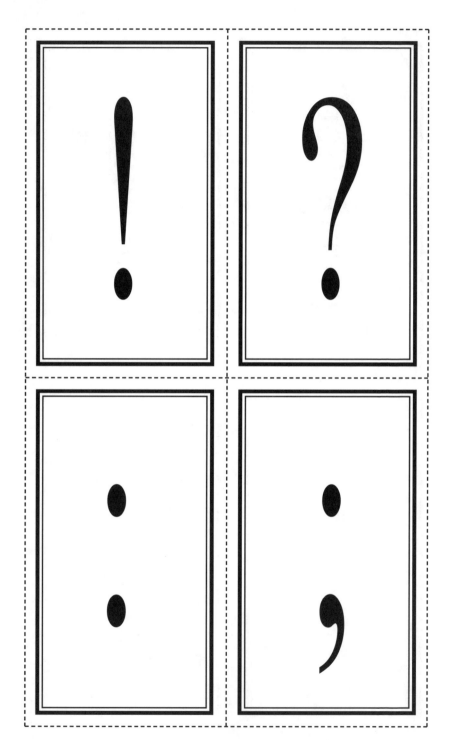

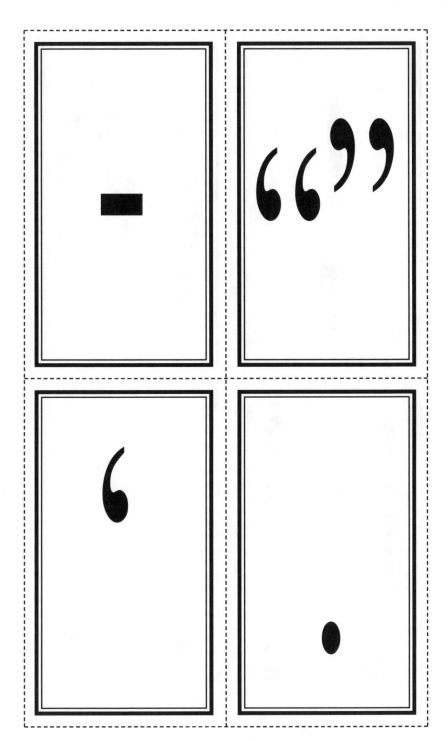

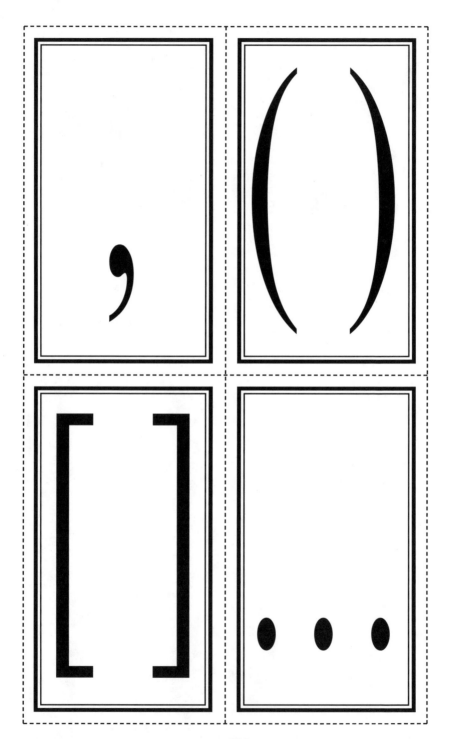

Punctuation Twister

Board construction directions

You will need:
  5'x 5' piece of plain cloth, felt or paper
  White glue or fabric glue
  Scissors
  Velcro™ (optional)

1. Photocopy the large punctuation marks on the following nine pages.

2. Cut out punctuation marks. You may use them as is or as a pattern to make felt or cloth punctuation marks.

3. Glue or use Velcro™ (for a felt game board) to attach the pieces to the game board. Place the pieces approximately twelve inches apart as shown in the example above.

If you are using a paper gameboard you may laminate the board before use. If using a felt or cloth board you may fold and place in a resealable storage bag for future use.

138

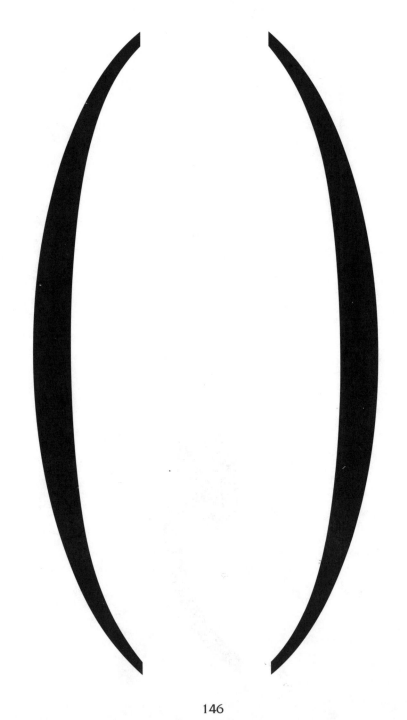

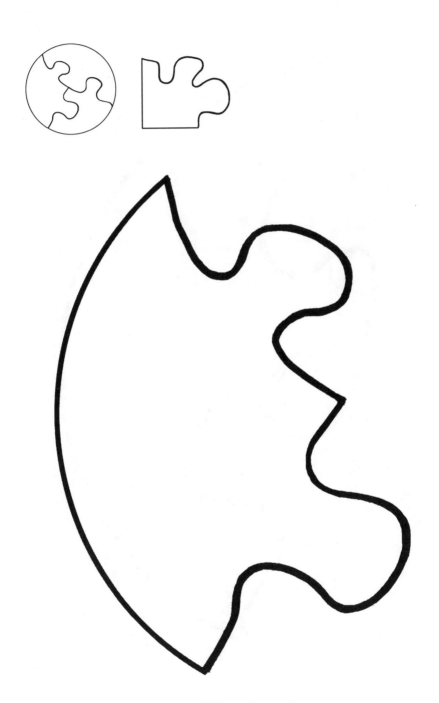

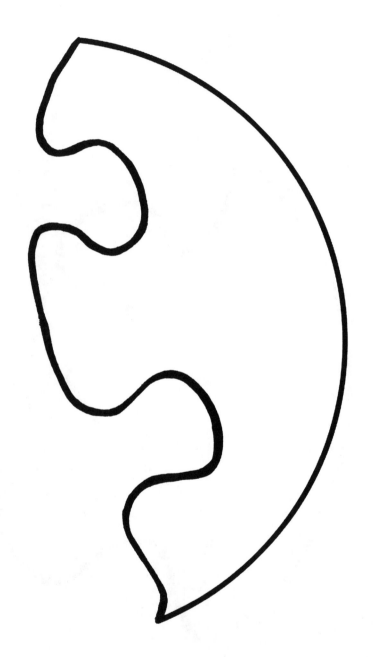

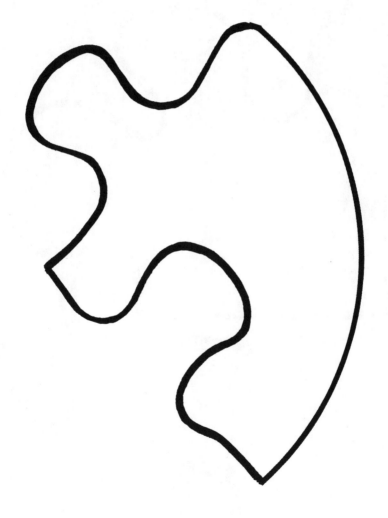

Who: Firefighter and "victim"

What: Arguing

When: During a demonstration

Where: A small classroom

Why: A rescue

Who: Short order cook and a waiter

What: Discussing making a sandwich

When: Lunch hour rush

Where: A French bistro

Why: Disagree about ingredients

Who: A tailor and a bridegroom

What: Measuring tuxedo pants

When: Morning of the wedding

Where: The church

Why: Bridegroom forgot to order

Who: Two Americans and two foreigners

What: Stuck in a broken elevator

When: Middle of the night

Where: In a hotel

Why: Trying to get to their rooms

Who: Police officer and two students

What: Getting a ticket

When: Middle of the school day

Where: A loud party

Why: Disturbing the peace

Who: Detective and suspect

What: Detective interrogating suspect

When: Midday

Where: Roller rink

Why: Suspect stole pair of in-line skates

Who: Hairstylist, mother, and son

What: Discussing a mohawk

When: Just before Bar Mitzvah

Where: Hair salon

Why: Mother wants it, son does not

Who: A bear and a hunter

What: Discussing the NRA

When: Over coffee

Where: A cabin in the woods

Why: Bear is running for office

Who: Psycho driver and two passengers

What: Heading toward a cliff

When: After driver's therapy

Where: On a bus

Why: Passengers are taunting driver

Who: Knight, princess, and dragon

What: Failed rescue attempt

When: Once upon a time

Where: Dragon's lair

Why: Princess likes the dragon

Who: Two pilgrims

What: Discussing dinner

When: The first Thanksgiving

Where: 17th century Massachusetts

Why: Turkey vs. grilled cheese

Who: Parent, child, and two friends

What: Planning to T.P. a house

When: After hearing a rumor

Where: At the supermarket

Why: Kids want parent to buy T.P.

Who: Valedictorian and the class "loser"

What: Talking about college

When: After graduation

Where: The principal's office

Why: Loser dared the other to "moon" class

Who: Senior citizens

What: Skydiving for the first time

When: After friend's funeral

Where: In the plane

Why: To get money from the will

Who: Two friends

What: Discussing a third friend

When: Before school

Where: Walking to school

Why: Third friend is being abused

Who: Boy and girl

What: Discussing teen pregnancy

When: After doctor's appointment

Where: In the car

Why: What to do? Who to tell?

Who: Two to four toddlers

What: Playing hide-and-seek

When: Before naptime

Where: The babysitter's house

Why: They're not tired

Who: Two sports fanatics

What: Rooting for opposing teams

When: During the Superbowl (or like)

Where: During a wedding reception

Why: Listening on headphones

Who: Two to four students

What: Taking down dance decorations

When: Afternoon of Homecoming

Where: School gym

Why: Students don't like the theme

Who: Prosecution and defense lawyers

What: Discussing a plea agreement

When: During a trial

Where: The judge's chambers

Why: Lawyers think judge is corrupt

Who: Two students
What: Acting as "fashion police"
When: While drinking lattes
Where: At the mall
Why: Making fun of people

Who: Eagle and a mouse
What: Discussing vegetarianism
When: Lunchtime
Where: The eagle's nest
Why: Mouse doesn't want to be eaten

Who: A parade of ants
What: Considering crossing the road
When: After stealing food
Where: Edge of picnic ground
Why: A car is coming

Who: Drug addict and supplier
What: Arguing
When: Late at night
Where: A dimly lit street corner
Why: Addict is trying to quit

1. Did Player 1 meet the objective?   yes   no
2. Did Player 2 meet the objective?   yes   no
3. Did Player 3 meet the objective?   yes   no
4. Which Player (who met the objective) performed most convincingly?

_____

1. Did Player 1 meet the objective?   yes   no
2. Did Player 2 meet the objective?   yes   no
3. Did Player 3 meet the objective?   yes   no
4. Which Player (who met the objective) performed most convincingly?

_____

1. Did Player 1 meet the objective?   yes   no
2. Did Player 2 meet the objective?   yes   no
3. Did Player 3 meet the objective?   yes   no
4. Which Player (who met the objective) performed most convincingly?

_____

1. Did Player 1 meet the objective?   yes   no
2. Did Player 2 meet the objective?   yes   no
3. Did Player 3 meet the objective?   yes   no
4. Which Player (who met the objective) performed most convincingly?

_____

1. Did Team 1 meet the objective? yes no
2. Did Team 2 meet the objective? yes no
3. Did Team 3 meet the objective? yes no
4. Which Team (who met the objective) performed most convincingly?

_____

---

1. Did Team 1 meet the objective? yes no
2. Did Team 2 meet the objective? yes no
3. Did Team 3 meet the objective? yes no
4. Which Team (who met the objective) performed most convincingly?

_____

---

1. Did Team 1 meet the objective? yes no
2. Did Team 2 meet the objective? yes no
3. Did Team 3 meet the objective? yes no
4. Which Team (who met the objective) performed most convincingly?

_____

---

1. Did Team 1 meet the objective? yes no
2. Did Team 2 meet the objective? yes no
3. Did Team 3 meet the objective? yes no
4. Which Team (who met the objective) performed most convincingly?

_____

Dollar Incentives

To follow is a page of reproducible Grammar Wars Dollar incentives. Teachers may or may not choose to incorporate them into the use of these games.

Many teachers use incentives to motivate, to show clear winners, and to teach responsibility. (You lose your dollar — it's gone.)

Grammar Wars Dollars may be used to purchase:
- bonus homework points
  (i.e. $5 = 5pts or $15 = free homework assignment)
- items at the school store
  (i.e. $5 = a pencil)
- items in a classroom store (teacher provides)
  (i.e. $5 = two lollipops)
- a class or team party
  (i.e. $100 = a pizza party)

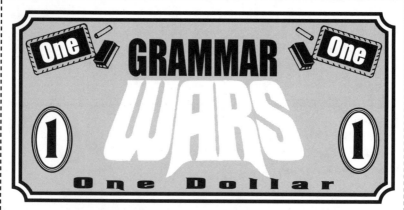

Appendix

Grade Level Matrix

Game	Page	Objective	K-3	4-6	7-8	9-12
Active Anachronisms	89	Editing			✔	✔
Adverts	82	Persuasive Appeals		✔	✔	✔
Allitterhyme	69	Listening	✔	✔		
All Together Now!	18	Spelling	✔	✔	✔	✔
All Together Now! II	32	Vocabulary	✔	✔	✔	✔
Alphabet Pairs	17	Alphabetical Order	✔	✔	✔	✔
Alphabet Poem	20	Alphabetical Order			✔	✔
Alphabet Race	19	Alphabetical Order	✔	✔		
Alphabet Race II	20	Alphabetical Order			✔	✔
Alphabet Scramble	18	Alphabetical Order	✔	✔		
Alphabetize	15	Alphabetical Order	✔	✔	✔	✔
Alpha-Parts	47	Alphabetical Order Parts of Speech			✔	✔
Bad Ad	82	Persuasive Appeals		✔	✔	✔
Beginnings and Endings	30	Phonics Affixes	✔	✔	✔	✔
Beginnings and Endings II	30	Affixes Vocabulary			✔	✔
Between the Lines	68	Connotation			✔	✔
Capital Flash	54	Capitals	✔	✔	✔	✔
Capital Idea!	52	Capitals	✔	✔	✔	✔
Chores	66	Listening Reading	✔	✔		
Chores II	66	Listening	✔	✔	✔	

Grade Level Matrix

Game	Page	Objective	K-3	4-6	7-8	9-12
Comma Along With Me	53	Comma Uses	✔	✔	✔	✔
Comma, Period, Out	56	Punctuation Marks			✔	✔
Compound It!	22	Vocabulary Phonics	✔	✔	✔	
Contraction Action	95	Contractions	✔	✔	✔	✔
Counting Clauses	46	Clauses			✔	✔
Describe It!	61	Complete Thoughts Vocabulary Adjectives	✔	✔		
Dialects	29	Vowels			✔	✔
Dictionary Race	91	Dictionary Skills	✔	✔	✔	✔
Difficult Duos	72	Reading Comprehension			✔	✔
Do It!	65	Reading		✔	✔	✔
Don't Get Tense	47	Verb Tenses			✔	✔
Down to Earth Narrative	81	Specific Detail		✔	✔	✔
Drop Out	40	Subject Verb Agreement			✔	✔
Drop Out II	41	Any Grammar or Punctuation Rule			✔	✔
Ears and Actions	71	Reading Comprehension	✔	✔	✔	✔

Grade Level Matrix

Game	Page	Objective	K-3	4-6	7-8	9-12
Edit It!	86	Coherence Organization Punctuation Grammar Spelling	✔	✔	✔	✔
Emotional Words	37	Vocabulary	✔	✔		
Endings Begin	27	Phonics		✔	✔	✔
End-Rhyme Scene	37	Vocabulary	✔	✔	✔	✔
Every Adjective	48	Adjectives	✔	✔	✔	✔
Exceptions Aloud	24	Pronunciation Vocabulary	✔	✔		
Family Reunion	24	Vocabulary Phonics	✔	✔		
Figure It Out!	94	Figurative Language		✔	✔	✔
Figures of Speech	95	Figurative Language		✔	✔	✔
Figure This	96	Figurative Language			✔	✔
Find It Fast!	91	Book Structure		✔	✔	✔
Finish Your Plate	30	Versatile Expression	✔	✔	✔	✔
First Line, Last Line	83	Everything			✔	✔
First Line, Last Line — Drop Outs	84	Grammar Rules			✔	✔
Fix This!	35	Affixes Vocabulary	✔	✔	✔	✔
Flash Dance	55	Punctuation		✔	✔	✔
Flip	93	Antonyms			✔	✔
Flip II	94	Antonyms			✔	✔

Grade Level Matrix

Game	Page	Objective	K-3	4-6	7-8	9-12
Forms and Features	92	Genres		✔	✔	✔
Form It	73	Narrative Structure Narrative Style		✔	✔	✔
Four-Sentence Scene	59	Sentence Types			✔	✔
General's Ladder, The	35	Vocabulary Connotation	✔	✔	✔	✔
Get Back in Line!	63	Grammar	✔	✔	✔	✔
Getting a Rise	76	Tone, Style		✔	✔	✔
Give Me Your Tone!	80	Vocal/Physical Tone			✔	✔
Greater Than or Equal To	28	Phonics			✔	✔
Half Thought/ Whole Thought	60	Complete Thoughts	✔	✔	✔	
Have You Seen My Modifier?	46	Modifiers			✔	✔
Homonee-Quips	36	Commonly Confused Words		✔	✔	✔
Homy-nuts	34	Commonly Confused words		✔	✔	✔
Honk	40	Parts of Speech		✔	✔	✔
Honk It!	39	Parts of Speech		✔	✔	✔
Human Sentences	70	Everything			✔	✔
I Hear …	92	Rhymes, Sounds, Onomatopoeia			✔	✔

Grade Level Matrix

Game	Page	Objective	K-3	4-6	7-8	9-12
I Know What You Meant	75	Listening			✔	✔
In Your Own Words	67	Listening Paraphrase Interpretation		✔	✔	✔
Jigsaw	62	Organization		✔	✔	✔
Junior College Bowl	65	Narrative Elements	✔	✔	✔	✔
Junior Sentence Types	61	Sentence Types	✔	✔	✔	
Keep 'Em Short	25	Syllables Vocabulary	✔	✔	✔	
Lead Letter	15	Vocabulary	✔			
Liar's Club	35	Roots Affixes		✔	✔	✔
Literalists	96	Figurative Language			✔	✔
Long and Short Race	27	Vowels	✔	✔		
Loud Letters	16	Phonics	✔	✔		
L.O.W.	45	Prepositions Adjectives			✔	✔
Magnet Words	32	Antonyms Synonyms	✔	✔	✔	✔
Mellow, Medium, Mad	33	Vocabulary		✔	✔	✔
Mix A Spell	18	Spelling Phonics	✔	✔		

166

Grade Level Matrix

Game	Page	Objective	K-3	4-6	7-8	9-12
Morphing	31	Phonics Alphabet Principle	✔	✔	✔	
My Life	75	Tone Vocabulary	✔	✔	✔	✔
Name That Sentence	59	Complete Thoughts Subjects and Verbs Varied Expression	✔	✔	✔	✔
Name That Sentence II	61	Sentence Types	✔	✔	✔	
Name That Sound	23	Reading Phonics	✔	✔		
New Words	25	Vocabulary Phonics	✔	✔	✔	✔
Noise	19	Alphabetical Order	✔	✔		
Not Quite Scene	83	Details			✔	✔
Now I'm Done	60	Complete Sentences			✔	✔
Now I'm Done II	60	Complete Sentences		✔	✔	✔
Obsession	99	Punctuation			✔	✔
Obsessionpux	58	Punctuation			✔	✔
Order in the Court!	80	Organization Details		✔	✔	✔
Paragraphic	85	Paragraphs Supporting Detail		✔	✔	✔
Para-linz	73	Parallelism		✔	✔	✔

Grade Level Matrix

Game	Page	Objective	K-3	4-6	7-8	9-12
Parts Expert	42	Parts of Speech		✔	✔	✔
Parts Idiot	42	Parts of Speech		✔	✔	✔
Parts of Speech Relay	48	Parts of Speech	✔	✔	✔	✔
Poets' Slaves	99	Punctuation Marks			✔	✔
Point of View	97	Points of View			✔	✔
Point the Part	39	Parts of Speech	✔	✔	✔	✔
Point the Plurals	91	Plurals		✔	✔	✔
Positive Amendment, A	90	Appositives			✔	✔
Predict the End	86	Developmental Reading			✔	✔
Punctuate This	51	Punctuation Marks	✔	✔	✔	✔
Punctuate Your Neighbor	53	Punctuation Marks		✔	✔	✔
Punctuation Ballet	51	Punctuation Marks			✔	✔
Punctuation Inferno	57	Punctuation Marks				✔
Punctuation Spasm	54	Punctuation Marks	✔	✔	✔	✔
Punctuation Twister	55	Punctuation Marks	✔	✔	✔	✔
Pyramid Story	62	Sentence Structures		✔	✔	✔
Quotes	54	Quotation Marks	✔	✔	✔	✔
Random Marks	56	Punctuation Marks		✔	✔	✔
RatioMinute	98	Vocabulary			✔	✔
Rhyme Race	22	Phonics Vocabulary	✔	✔	✔	✔

Grade Level Matrix

Game	Page	Objective	K-3	4-6	7-8	9-12
Rhyme Race II	22	Phonics Vocabulary	✔	✔	✔	✔
Root Repeat	34	Roots		✔	✔	✔
Rumor	71	Reading Comprehension		✔	✔	✔
Scavenger Hunt	92	Book Structure		✔	✔	✔
Scene with ... or Scene without ...	50	Everything			✔	✔
Scene without a Word	43	Parts of Speech		✔	✔	✔
Sentence Charade	59	Vocabulary Complete Thoughts	✔	✔		
Sentence Rotations	64	Sentence Types			✔	✔
Sentence Scramble	88	Sentence Structure			✔	✔
Short or Long?	23	Vowels	✔	✔	✔	
Show Me More!	76	Description Detail	✔	✔	✔	✔
Sounds Like	23	Elements of Style	✔	✔	✔	✔
Speak!	82	Organization		✔	✔	✔
Speech Spasm	77	Organization			✔	✔
Speeds	74	Verb Tenses			✔	✔
Speed Reader	67	Reading	✔	✔	✔	✔
Speed Reader II	68	Reading	✔	✔	✔	
Spell-Well Letter Number	17	Spelling		✔	✔	✔

Grade Level Matrix

Game	Page	Objective	K-3	4-6	7-8	9-12
Spelled Out	98	Spelling			✔	✔
Spot the Hidden Letter	28	Phonics			✔	✔
Stand and Deliver	45	Empty Bucket		✔	✔	✔
Start and Stop	51	Punctuation Marks		✔	✔	✔
Start with a Letter	15	Vocabulary Spelling	✔	✔	✔	✔
Story, Story, Out (Audience Styles)	79	Tone, Style		✔	✔	✔
Story, Story, Out (Point of View)	79	Point of View			✔	✔
Story, Story, Out (Prose Styles)	78	Prose Styles		✔	✔	✔
Story Structure	68	Narrative Structure Listening		✔	✔	✔
Sumo Sentences	86	Versatility of Expression		✔	✔	✔
Switch	41	Subject Verb Agreement			✔	✔
Sybil	36	Words with Multiple Meanings		✔	✔	✔
Syllable Count	24	Syllables Phonics	✔	✔	✔	
Syllable Scene	25	Syllables			✔	✔
Tense Exchanges	47	Verb Tenses			✔	✔

Grade Level Matrix

Game	Page	Objective	K-3	4-6	7-8	9-12
Tense Scene	43	Verb Tenses			✔	✔
Thesis Thought	89	Theses			✔	✔
This Part Only!	40	Parts of Speech	✔	✔	✔	✔
To Be or Not To Be	42	"To Be" Forms		✔	✔	✔
Transition Position	87	Transitions			✔	✔
Truth or Fiction?	76	Communication Complete Thoughts	✔	✔	✔	
Turret Trade-Off or Spastic Story Time	84	Punctuation Marks			✔	✔
Upper-Lower Case	16	Penmanship Cases of Letters	✔	✔		
Verb Wars	44	Verb Types			✔	✔
Vocabulary Ladder	93	Vocabulary Spelling	✔	✔	✔	✔
Vocabulary Relay	38	Vocabulary		✔	✔	✔
Voice-Over with Punctuation	57	Punctuation Marks			✔	✔
Voices	77	Passive and Active Voices			✔	✔
Voracious Vocabulary	38	Vocabulary			✔	✔
Vowel Scene	26	Vowels		✔	✔	✔
What Are You After?	80	Purposes		✔	✔	✔
What It Is!	66	Letters, Words, Sentences	✔	✔		

Grade Level Matrix

Game	Page	Objective	K-3	4-6	7-8	9-12
What's Missing?	69	Letter Format		✔	✔	✔
What's the Form?	65	Organization		✔	✔	✔
What's the Point?	85	Reading Listening Main Point		✔	✔	✔
Where to Begin	44	Parts of Speech		✔	✔	✔
Which Witch Is Which?	63	Clauses			✔	✔
Why'd It Happen?	67	Listening	✔	✔	✔	✔
Word Match	33	Reading Phonics	✔	✔		
Word Sort	31	Grouping	✔	✔	✔	
Write Right!	85	Capitals Periods Spacing	✔	✔		
Yours and Mime	74	Details		✔	✔	✔

Vocabulary

Accept:	To believe and play with a thing or idea offered into a scene.
Advance:	To increase the energy in a performed action. The "Advance" can take an action from barely noticeable, to realism, to absurd.
Block:	To undo (recreate into something else) consciously an offer from another player.
CROWE:	Character, Relationship, Objective, Where, Emotion/condition.
Drive:	To force only your ideas on another player in a scene.
Doneygraph	A chart structure, usually placed on the floor with a box-matrix printed on it. In each box is a word or symbol to be used by the participants. I first saw this learning tool used by Jan Doney from northern California.
Duet Poem:	Two players improvise a poem alternating one line at a time. The lines should rhyme and have matching rhythms.
Five Ws:	The Method acting version of CROWE (Where, When, Who, What, and Why).
Focus:	The point to which attention is drawn on-stage.
Form, The:	Narrative in Improv (routine, problem, routine, new routine).
Give and Take:	Bringing the focus to yourself and then letting another player have it in a scene.
Justify:	To treat a "mistake" as if it had been intended.
Narrative:	The structural sequence of a story being told/performed.
New Routine:	The new pattern that has evolved out of the hero's exchange with the problem and the solution in a narrative.
Offer:	To present a thing or idea into a scene as if it were real.
Physical Conversation:	A scene between two players where only one mimes at a time while the partner freezes. No words are spoken: The actions convey "lines" between the two characters.
Platform:	The information at the beginning of a narrative from which all following elements must come.
Problem:	The problem that interrupts the routine.
Reincorporation:	The appearance or reappearance of things, or the logical appearance of items/behaviors out of the previously established information.
Routine:	The opening action that is the hero's natural pattern.
Solution:	The action that dissolves the problem state.
Word-at-a-Time:	Sentences spoken by two or more players, each speaking only one word at a time.

Resources

Games and Exercises:

Improvisation Through Theatresports™, Belt and Stockley
Thespis Productions
2010 12th Ave. S.E.
Puyallup, WA 98372

Improvisation for the Theater, Spolin
Northwestern University Press
1735 Benson Ave.
Evanston, IL
ISBN # 0-8101-0018-5

Playbook, Fourth Ed., BATS (Get the latest edition)
Bay Area Theatresports™
P.O. Box 884192
San Francisco, CA 94188
(415) 824-8220

IMPRO, Johnstone
Theatre Arts Books
29 West 35th Street
New York, NY 10001

Comic Structure and Narrative

The Comic Toolbox, Vorhaus
Silman-James Press
Distributed by Samuel French Trade
7623 Sunset Blvd.
Hollywood, CA 90046

Academic Content Standards

California State Content Standards in Language Arts
http://www.cde.ca.gov/challenge/standards/LangHTML/contents.html

About the Author

Tom Ready has been teaching theatre and language arts for the past twenty years at Lassen High School, Lassen Community College, Chico State, and within the Arts-in-Corrections program at CCC Susanville, and High Desert State Prison. He has worked as a theatre consultant for the California Arts Project, the Northeast California Arts Project, and various counties in northern California. He presents workshops, consults, and is a conference speaker with educational and state organizations in the areas of team building, restructuring, and systems thinking.

He enjoys producing original theatrical works, in recent years working with Snail Records in Chicago on a production of Ken Nordine's *Word Jazz*, and Ruth Gendler's *The Book of Qualities*.

In 1990 he appeared in a Malpaso production of Clint Eastwood's *Pink Cadillac* with Bernadette Peters.

He recently finished a collaborative theatre project with Dr. William Torch, pediatric neurologist at Washoe Medical Center in Reno, Nevada, on an original script about child abuse and children's rights presented at Lassen High School.

Tom was awarded a national Christa McAuliffe Fellowship for the 1997-98 school year in the areas of drama, literacy, and educational restructuring.

Currently, Tom teaches acting and English, and is in charge of organizational development at Lassen High School in Susanville, California.

Order Form

Meriwether Publishing Ltd.
P.O. Box 7710
Colorado Springs, CO 80933
Telephone: (719) 594-4422
Website: www.meriwetherpublishing.com

TM

Please send me the following books:

_____ **Grammar Wars #BK-B241**   **$15.95**
by Tom Ready
179 games and improvs for learning language arts

_____ **Improve with Improv! #BK-B160**   **$14.95**
by Brie Jones
A guide to improvisation and character development

_____ **Theatre Games for Young Performers #BK-B188**   **$16.95**
by Maria C. Novelly
Improvisations and exercises for developing acting skills

_____ **Theatre Games and Beyond #BK-B217**   **$16.95**
by Amiel Schotz
A creative approach for performers

_____ **Let's Put on a Show! #BK-B231**   **$16.95**
by Adrea Gibbs
A beginner's theatre handbook for young actors

_____ **Winning Monologs for Young Actors #BK-B127** **$15.95**
by Peg Kehret
Honest-to-life monologs for young actors

_____ **Everything About Theatre! #BK-B200**   **$17.95**
by Robert L. Lee
The guidebook of theatre fundamentals

These and other fine Meriwether Publishing books are available at
your local bookstore or direct from the publisher. Prices subject to
change without notice. Check our website or call for current prices.

Name: _____

Organization name: _____

Address: _____

City: _____ State: _____

Zip: _____ Phone: _____

❏ **Check enclosed**

❏ **Visa / MasterCard / Discover #** _____

Signature: _____
Expiration date: _____

(required for Visa/MasterCard/Discover orders)

Colorado residents: Please add 3% sales tax.
Shipping: Include $2.75 for the first book and 50¢ for each additional book ordered.

❏ *Please send me a copy of your complete catalog of books and plays.*